AF510111

After Effort

What Comes Next When Struggle Stops Working

Kim Aronson

Copyright © 2026 by Kim Aronson

All rights reserved.

Disclaimer: This book is intended as a guide and an informational resource only. It is not a substitute for professional advice, diagnosis, or treatment. If you believe you are experiencing emotional, mental, or physical health issues, please consult a qualified psychologist, doctor, or other healthcare professional for personalized guidance and support.

Contents

About The Author 157

Kim Aronson

PART I

WHY EASE FEELS LIKE CHEATING

Chapter One

The Moment It Gets Easy

The document was supposed to take two weeks. You knew the shape of this work — you'd done versions of it before. Fourteen days of mornings, the slow accumulation of pages, the familiar frustration of finding the right word, the sentence that wouldn't sit right no matter how many times you rewrote it. By day ten you'd usually hit the wall where everything felt thin and borrowed. By day thirteen, you'd retrieve it. That was the rhythm. That was how you knew you were actually working.

This time you started on a Tuesday.

By Thursday afternoon, it was done.

Not the first draft kind of done. The kind where you read it back and the thought count felt right, the examples landed, the voice was there. The transitions didn't limp. You'd even caught yourself making small choices — cutting a paragraph that was fine but unnecessary, adding a line that changed the tone of a whole section. The decisions felt like yours. The work felt like yours. And something in your chest had gone still.

Not happy still. Confused still.

You sat with the document open. Read it again. Looked for the part where it broke, where the seams showed, where you'd gotten lazy and let something slide. Nothing. It held. It held better, maybe, than things that had taken you longer. The pages turned easily. The argument built. Someone could read this and follow you.

So why did it feel like cheating?

The first thought was a small one, the kind you barely notice passing through. *Something is wrong with me.* Not wrong as in broken, but wrong as in — you have lost something. Calibration. Standards. The ability to push yourself properly because if it came this easily, you must not have pushed at all. The effort-value equation, though you didn't have a name for it yet, had already solved itself in your nervous system before your conscious mind caught up. No struggle equals no real work. No real work means the output is suspect. The output is suspect means you are suspect.

You closed the laptop.

* * *

The day was clear outside. You had made coffee that morning and hadn't finished it, and it sat on the desk beside you, gone cold enough that the surface had formed a thin film. You picked it up. Put it down. Picked it up again. Your shoulders were high — when had they risen? They were nearly at your ears, and you consciously pressed them down, and felt them rise again within seconds. The body knows something before the mind arrives at it. The body was already arguing with the thing you'd just created.

This is what disorientation feels like when it lives in the nervous system instead of the mind. It doesn't announce itself as confusion. It announces itself as a problem in the shoulder blade. A tightness in the jaw. The held breath that you only notice when you try to breathe normally and find there's no room. The body is arguing with a conclusion the mind hasn't even formed yet.

You stood up. Walked to the window. The light outside was the particular slant of late afternoon in a season that isn't quite spring. There was a length to the shadows that meant the sun was moving toward something. Your neck was sore. When had you tensed your neck? You rolled your shoulders backward, trying to move whatever this was — this thing you couldn't name — down and out of your body. It didn't move. It settled into a new position. Your lower back. Your hands, suddenly aware of being hands, tingling faintly at the fingertips.

The competence had arrived while you were paying attention to the work itself and not paying attention to the fact that your nervous system was rewiring. This was the thing no one had warned you about. Everyone talked about the moment of achievement as though it would feel like something — like arrival, like landing, like the moment a plane stops climbing and levels off. But the nervous system doesn't experience achievement. It experiences the absence of what it used to feel. The nervous system experiences *loss*.

* * *

There is a particular disorientation that arrives when the work stops feeling like work.

Not in the sense of pleasure, though there can be that. Not in the sense of finally catching the wave of your own competence, though that's what you'd assume it would feel like if you'd ever really thought about it. The disorientation is sharper than that. It's the moment when the drama drains out of the effort and you suddenly realize you'd been using the drama as the proof. Struggle was the evidence that something real was happening. When the struggle evaporated, so did your permission to believe in what you'd done.

For years before this moment — maybe your whole life before this moment — you carried an assumption about how competence would announce itself. You thought it would feel like breaking through something. A crescendo. The moment where the weight finally gives and you can stand up straight. A triumph you'd recognize immediately, probably audibly. At minimum, you'd feel it in your chest. Relief, maybe. Pride. The satisfaction of having overcome.

But competence, when it actually arrives, doesn't tend to do that.

It arrives quietly. The way altitude changes when you're driving through a mountain pass — you don't notice the moment the pressure shifts in your ears. You don't see the trees get smaller or the air get thinner. You just look up and the landmarks are gone. The landmarks you'd been using to know where you were, to know if you were headed the right direction, to know if you were still doing the thing you'd meant to do. And suddenly they're not there, and the body has no reference points, and you start to suspect you've gone in a circle. You've lost the way. You're not actually climbing anymore because climbing would *feel* like climbing and this just feels like standing still.

The body was designed to trust sensation. Pain means something is wrong. Resistance means you're pushing against something real. The struggle is the reality check. When the resistance goes quiet, the nervous system spins out. Nothing to grip. Nothing to push against. No feedback except the feedback that says — yes, this is done, yes, it's good — and that feedback is so quiet it feels like nothing at all.

Annie Dillard talks about a ratchet that tightens in your back when you're doing real work, when you're holding yourself to something. You can feel that ratchet. You can point to it. It's in your shoulder blade, your lower spine, the exact place where you hold your doubt. When you're really trying, that tightness is constant. It's proof. The moment the tightness dissolves, the moment you move through a task without that particular strain, the mind doesn't trust it. The mind wants the strain. The mind is convinced the strain is the work.

Consider the person at the conference — the one you overheard at the coffee station, talking about finishing a document in what used to take weeks. *I'm terrified it's not good,* she said to someone she clearly didn't know very well, the kind of thing you only say to a stranger because you'll never see them again. *It came too fast. I can't find the part where I actually did the work.* The person she was talking to — someone who clearly still struggled the old way — tried to reassure her. Congratulated her. But the woman kept shaking her head. *That's just it. I don't feel like I've done anything. It doesn't feel like I deserve to claim it.*

This is competence in a body that's been trained to recognize struggle as the evidence of reality.

* * *

The guilt that comes next is strange because it doesn't announce itself as guilt. It arrives as a problem with math.

If the output is the same or better, but the input was radically less, then something doesn't add up. The equation that's been running in the background of your whole life says: great work equals great effort. Therefore, if the work is great and the effort was minimal, then something is being hidden. Either the work isn't actually great, or you're not seeing where the effort went, or — and this is the one the body really seizes on — you're doing something wrong.

You could call this the work-effort equation. It is brutally simple. It is also nearly impossible to live with when it fails to resolve.

The guilt is not the kind that makes you want to do better. It's the kind that makes you want to hide. If you let people see that something only took you two hours, they'll know you're lazy. If it only took two hours and it's actually good, they'll know you've been holding back all along, that you could have been producing like this the whole time and you were just choosing not to. The guilt is retrospective. It reframes every piece of work that took you a long time and makes you wonder if that was because you were thorough or because you were slow.

A person arrives at a place in their own competence and the first instinct is to keep it quiet.

Not out of humility. Out of fear that if the secret is out, the easy will stop being easy. As long as you're believing in your own struggle, as long as you're performing struggle for yourself and possibly for others, the competence stays reliable. The moment you admit that it came easily, you've somehow jinxed it. The ease will evaporate. You'll go back to the two-week version, and then you'll have to spend the next two weeks explaining why you've gotten worse at something you used to be good at.

So the guilt sits quietly. It sits in the same place the strain used to sit. It's a different kind of tension, but it's tension, and tension is at least familiar. The body prefers guilt to the unmoored feeling of having done something well and not knowing how you did it. Because if you don't know how you did it, how can you do it again? And if you can't do it again, then maybe it wasn't real in the first place.

The logic folds back on itself. The guilt is proof something is wrong with you. The proof that something is wrong is the ease itself. The ease is evidence that you're not really trying. Trying is what makes work matter. Therefore, the work doesn't matter. You don't trust yourself, and you have the guilt to prove it.

Think of the manager you know — the one who suddenly realized that their team was doing their best work in the months after they'd stopped micromanaging. The guilt was so sharp that she almost started managing more strictly again, just to make sure things were actually getting done, just to prove to herself that her absence of control was worth it. She caught herself at the edge of that decision. That's how close it was. The guilt nearly convinced her to destroy the conditions under which the best work was happening, just so she could feel like she was responsible for it.

* * *

There is a specific moment in the history of doing your own work — any work, but especially creative work, intellectual work, anything that comes from you and bears your fingerprints — when the resistance drops away and you realize you've actually learned something.

It's not victory. It's stranger than that.

You have been pushed against the same shape of problem so many times that your hands have learned it. Your mind has learned the topology. You don't have to think about where to hold anymore because your hands already know where they go. The learning is so deep that it's become invisible. You moved past the stage where you could feel yourself learning and into the stage where the learning is just running, underneath, like your heart beating. You don't have to concentrate on the heartbeat for it to keep going.

Mastery is the disappearance of your own effort from your own awareness.

This is, paradoxically, exactly when you become most suspicious of yourself.

Because for years before this moment, you could feel yourself learning. Every new technique was obvious as it arrived. Every small improvement was something you could point to. *I learned this.* The learning was an addition. It was something you could witness yourself acquiring, and the witnessing was a form of control. You knew what you knew because you could remember the moment you knew it.

But the deeper learning, the kind that turns into actual competence, stops announcing itself. It integrates itself. It becomes you instead of something you're carrying. And from the inside, that feels like nothing. That feels like you haven't changed at all. You're the same person, thinking the same thoughts, except suddenly the thoughts are organized in a way that produces a good result. The person at your desk is the person who's always been at your desk. The difference is in the tissues now, in the cellular memory, in the patterns that run without your permission.

The air is thinner and you don't notice the air because you're inside the air. You only notice the air when it changes again, and by then you're somewhere else and you can't go back to check what you were breathing before.

Your body knows something has shifted, though. That's where the disorientation lives. The nervous system registers the absence of the familiar resistance. The sympathetic charge that used to pulse through the work is gone. The work is parasympathetic now — easy, settled, not emergency. But the nervous system was trained to recognize emergency as realness. Without the emergency, it doesn't know what it's looking at. Without the struggle, it can't verify that you exist.

There's a writer who described it this way — and she wasn't talking about anything theoretical. She was describing the actual moment she sat down to write something that should have been hard and found that it wasn't. *I kept waiting to hit the wall,* she said. *The wall was always there. It was like an old friend. And then it wasn't there anymore, and I realized I'd been using the wall to know where I was. Without the wall, I don't know if I'm going forward or standing still. I don't know if anything is actually happening. I could be writing the best thing I've ever written or I could be sleepwalking. The ease doesn't tell me which.*

* * *

Struggle is dramatic. Struggle announces itself. Struggle has a shape, a narrative.

There is a problem, there is your effort against the problem, and there is the moment when either you or the problem gives way. That narrative is so ancient, so woven into the way we understand meaning, that we've started to assume the narrative *is* the meaning. The drama is the proof.

Ease has no narrative. Ease is what happens when the narrative has already been written somewhere else, in your tissues and your intuition and your hands, and now the story is just being transcribed. There is nothing for you to push against. There is nothing for the reader to push against vicariously. There is just the result, clean and quiet, with no visible evidence of its own making.

We live in a culture that worships at the altar of struggle. We have built an entire architecture of meaning around the idea that things that matter must be hard. The harder the thing, the more meaningful it is. An easier path is a lesser path. If you're not suffering, you're not learning. If you're not tired, you're not working hard enough. If you're not drained, you're cheating yourself.

This is why so many people, when they finally break through to competence, feel more like failures than they did when they were still learning.

The learning phase has all the drama. The learning phase is full of obvious obstacles and obvious victories and obvious growth. You can see it happening. You can feel it happening. The struggle is material. It's real. You can point to the problem you solved, the time you wasted, the evening you sat with your hands in your hair because the thing refused to work. That's all evidence. That's all proof. You earned something. You can see the shape of what you earned because it was hard to get.

But competence is invisible from the inside. The only way you know you've arrived is by the absence of something. The absence of the struggle that used to be there. The absence of the doubt that used to need managing. The absence of the night-sweats that used to come with putting anything out into the world that had your name on it. These absences feel like nothing. They feel like you've stopped trying. They feel like you've gotten lazy and the fall will come later, when someone finally notices that the emperor has no clothes.

So you keep working as if the struggle is still there. You keep pushing as if you need to push. You keep second-guessing as if second-guessing is still a necessary part of the process. You manufacture friction where none exists naturally, just so you can still believe in the work you're doing.

A hand pressed flat against a table. A jaw held tight. The held breath. The shoulders that won't stay down. These are not the feelings of someone doing their best work. These are the feelings of someone who doesn't trust that they've already arrived.

And the worst part: the manufactured friction works. The work gets worse. The output gets slower. The disorientation eases because now there's struggle again, now there's drama again, now the nervous system can verify that something real is happening. You've traded competence for the feeling of competence, and the trade feels like recovery.

* * *

For many people reading this, there is one more layer to this disorientation. There is one more reason why the ease feels not like achievement but like theft.

The work finished in two hours instead of two weeks. The quality is the same or better. And somewhere in that acceleration, in that impossible compression of time, there is an AI somewhere in the loop. Either in the research, or in the first draft, or in the editing, or in the fact that the AI has trained you to think differently about the problem so that when you sat down, you already knew what you wanted to say in a way you never did before. The AI is not visible in the final output, probably. The thinking is still yours. The voice is still yours. The choice to keep something or cut something is still yours. But the ease is not entirely yours, and suddenly the guilt is sharper because now there is a culprit. The culprit is the tool. The tool has cheated you out of your struggle.

This is a particular disorientation for this moment in time. People who are just now encountering what it feels like to produce something good with dramatically less resistance are running into an equipment problem disguised as a moral problem. The equipment has changed. The resistance is gone. The body is telling them that the resistance was the proof of worth, so the absence of resistance is proof of the absence of worth. But what if the absence of resistance is just proof that the equipment has changed?

What if ease is not a sign that something is wrong, but a sign that something has shifted in the conditions under which work happens?

This doesn't resolve the disorientation. It just names it more accurately. The disorientation remains. The body still doesn't know how to feel about the absence of strain. The guilt is still there, now with a new target, a new place to attach the suspicion. Maybe the guilt was always going to be there. Maybe every time ease arrives, in any context, the nervous system will push back. Maybe this is just what it feels like to become competent in a world that has always taught you that competence should hurt.

A woman in a workshop described what happened when she let herself believe — just for an afternoon — that the easy way of working was legitimate. She didn't have to maintain the fiction of struggle anymore. She could work the way her body actually worked, which was efficiently. Her output tripled in three weeks. The quality stayed consistent. And the voice she found in that efficiency was clearer than anything she'd written before. She brought a piece of it to a writing group, and someone asked how long it had taken her. She told them. The moment the words left her mouth, she watched their face recalibrate. *Oh,* they said. Just that. Just *oh.* And she felt the shift — the moment her work went from impressive to suspicious. The moment ease stopped being a skill and started being a shortcut. She didn't go back to struggling deliberately, but she did something worse. She started padding her work with unnecessary complexity, just to signal that real effort had been involved. The work got worse. It got less clear. It took longer. And when people asked how long it had taken her that time, she had an answer that made sense in the world they all shared. A world where struggle is the evidence of care.

That's what the disorientation can do if you let it run. It can convince you to sabotage your own best capabilities in order to stay legible to people who believe that hard work should feel hard.

* * *

You open the document again. It's still there. It's still done. It's still good. The shoulders are still high. The jaw is still tight. The coffee is cold. The body hasn't solved the problem of the absence of struggle. The body probably won't solve it this time, or the next time, or the time after that. Every time ease arrives, the nervous system will have to learn again what ease actually is. Not laziness. Not the absence of care. Not evidence of insufficiency. Just ease. Just the way the work feels when the learning has already done its work underneath.

The mind knows this. The mind can understand the logic of it. But the mind lives in a body, and the body remembers what it was taught. The body learned that strain is proof, that effort is evidence, that struggle is the price of anything worth doing.

What happens when the price gets paid somewhere else — in the past, in the practice, in the accumulated repetition that the body has absorbed so completely that it's invisible now? What happens when you arrive somewhere and the road behind you has dissolved so entirely that you can't even see the distance you traveled to get there?

The document still sits on the screen. It is done. It is good. Your hands are trembling slightly, the way they do when you're not sure if you should feel relief or grief.

Chapter Two

Effort–Value Fusion

The boy is nine years old, bent over his math homework at the kitchen table. He gets a problem wrong. Not because he doesn't understand it—he does—but because his hand moved too quickly and he misread the number. His mother appears in the doorway with the coffee that isn't for him. She glances at the page.

"Did you try hard on this one?" she asks.

This is not a neutral question. They both know it. He nods. She puts her hand on his shoulder. "That's what matters," she says. "You did your best."

The problem is still wrong. But something in his body shifts. He feels the warmth of her hand. He feels, for a moment, safe. The wrong answer doesn't matter as much as the rightness of the effort. As long as he tried, he belongs in this house. As long as he tried, he is worthy of her attention.

Thirty years later, this boy—now a woman, now an executive who hasn't sat at a kitchen table in decades—will feel a familiar tremor in her chest when someone tells her to stop working so hard. The tremor is small. She barely notices it. But her body remembers what it learned: that ease is the opposite of love. That stopping is abandonment. That the moment she stops trying, she might disappear.

* * *

The effort–value fusion is installed early and installed everywhere. It doesn't arrive as a rule you can read. It arrives as a feeling, a texture, a pattern in how the people you depend on look at you and look away. It arrives as praise and as safety.

It arrives as the invisible price of belonging.

A child who is praised for her grade gets one kind of message. A child who is praised for how hard she studied—who is told "I can see how much effort you put in" when she brings home a B+ and her teacher marked the mistake in red—gets something else entirely. One is conditional on outcome. The other is conditional on struggle. One teaches that what you produce matters. The other teaches that what you endure matters more.

The distinction seems small. The psychic effect reaches into everything the child will become.

By age twelve, the child has learned something about the architecture of worth. She has learned that struggle is legible. It can be seen, measured, respected. Success without visible toil is suspicious. If it came too easily, it doesn't count. If you weren't tired, you didn't care enough. The body becomes a proof of faith.

In the ninth grade, a girl stays up until midnight working on a social studies project. The poster is neat, colorful, well-researched. She gets an A. Her father sees the dark circles under her eyes. "You really put in the work," he says. His face softens. His hand finds her head. "I'm proud of how much you care." The moment is small but it lodges somewhere. She files it away. Next project, she will work until midnight again, not because the work requires it, but because the love does.

In the same grade, another girl completes an equally strong project in two hours. She reads the material once, understands it, puts it together with efficiency and creativity. She gets an A. Her mother glances at it, says "nice job," and moves on. The girl feels something small shrivel. It was too easy. The grade doesn't count because she wasn't depleted. She decides, without words, that she will need to prove herself differently. She will find harder things. She will work longer. She will make sure there is evidence of her struggle. The A was a fluke. The love was withheld. She will earn it next time.

This is not about laziness or virtue. This is about a child learning the invisible grammar of her family. The rules are written not in instruction but in who gets attention, who gets touched, whose effort gets remarked upon. A child who grows up being praised for her trying learns to equate worth with struggle. Another child, equally diligent, learns that effort should be invisible—that the goal is to make it look effortless. Both are distorted. Both are learning that human value is somehow conditional on how they perform.

But it is the child praised for her effort who enters adulthood with the deepest fusion. She has been trained to believe that trying hard is the moral good. That rest is laziness. That if something didn't cost her something, it doesn't matter.

* * *

In families where responsibility arrives early, the equation doesn't just settle in—it calcifies into something more urgent, more absolute. The parentified child—the one who learned to read her mother's mood from the set of her shoulders, who translated the parents' arguments into manageable stories, who managed the household before she could reach the top shelf of the cupboard, who held the infrastructure of family feeling in her small hands—learns something beyond a work ethic. She learns that her value is directly proportional to her usefulness. She learns that she is the reason her mother doesn't fall apart. She is the reason the house runs. She is the reason there is any oxygen in the family system at all.

For her, effort is not optional. It is the price of safety, the price of love, the price of existence in this family. To rest is to let the family collapse. To ask for help is to betray your mother. To be sick is a luxury for people whose parents can afford to take care of them.

These children do not develop a work ethic. They develop an arrangement with survival.

A woman is seven years old, watching her mother's face after a difficult call from her grandmother. The mother has been quiet all evening, her movements slowed. The father is at work. There is no one here but this small child and the mother's grief, which sits on the kitchen table like a third person. The daughter knows—children know these things in their nervous systems, before they know them in words—that her mother is suffering. The light in her eyes has dimmed. So the daughter climbs down from the couch. She clears the dinner dishes without being asked, a task that takes both hands and all her concentration. She draws a picture and leaves it on the table. She is very, very good. She doesn't ask for a snack. She doesn't interrupt. She makes herself small and useful. When her mother finally turns to her, the mother's eyes are a little brighter. She pulls her daughter into her lap. For a moment the mother is more present, more here. The daughter's small body understands: your effort is what brings people back. Your effort is what makes people love you instead of disappearing into their sadness.

For the rest of her life, this woman will feel this arrangement in her bones. She will work until her shoulders ache. She will ignore the email that doesn't need a response tonight, and then answer it anyway because not answering will feel like a small act of abandonment. She will take on the extra project even though she's already exhausted. She will run on empty and call it commitment. And underneath all of it, though she will not be able to articulate this until much later, she will feel it: that if she stops, the people she loves will fall. That her rest is a betrayal. That her body is not hers—it is the mechanism that keeps the people she depends on from drowning.

The effort is not about accomplishment. It is about magic. It is about control. It is about the illusion that if she just tries hard enough, she can protect people she cannot protect. She can fix what is broken. She can make sure no one ever has to suffer the way her mother suffered. Her labor becomes a kind of prayer, not to God but to the universe: take my exhaustion instead of taking them.

This is the equation, and it is absolute: effort equals value equals safety equals love.

For the parentified child grown into an adult, rest is not just unpleasant—it is existentially threatening. To be at rest is to be useless. To be useless is to be unlovable. To be unlovable is to be at the mercy of the family's dissolution. The body tenses against this at every opportunity.

* * *

Somewhere in adolescence, this fusion transforms. It stops being something the child does and becomes something the child is. A "hard worker." A "responsible one." A "serious person." These become self-concepts, and self-concepts are armor. They are proof of legitimacy. They are the answer to the question that lives in every adolescent's nervous system: Am I okay? Am I normal? Do I belong?

If I am someone who works hard, then yes. Yes to all of it.

The self-concept settles into place like concrete. It becomes difficult to distinguish from the person's actual being. A teenager with this identity begins to organize her entire life around maintaining it. She takes the harder classes. She joins activities. She volunteers. Not because these things call to her, but because they are proof. They are evidence. They are the documentation of her worthiness.

She notices, vaguely, that other kids seem to rest more easily. That they do assignments and move on. That they fail sometimes and don't seem to interpret failure as evidence of their fundamental unworthiness. But she interprets their ease as luck, not as freedom. They probably have easier lives. They probably don't understand what it costs to matter.

By the time these people reach adulthood, the equation has become so naturalized that they cannot see it. Effort is not something they chose. It is the ground they walk on. It is the air. Everyone works hard, they assume. Or at least, everyone serious does. Everyone who matters. Everyone who is worthy of respect, of love, of taking up space in the world.

When someone suggests they could delegate, or take a day off, or work four days a week, their nervous system registers this as a threat. Not because of the logistics but because of the identity. To delegate is to admit you are not capable. To take a day off is to suggest you don't care enough. To work less is to become less. The suggestion lands in the body as a kind of moral accusation.

A woman in her mid-forties is offered a leadership position that would require less hands-on work. She would delegate more. She would manage rather than produce. She should be relieved. Instead, she feels something sharp in her chest. When she imagines this role, she feels her value drain away. Who would she be if she wasn't the person who does the work? Who would she be if she wasn't the one solving the problem at midnight? She turns down the job, tells herself it wasn't aligned with her values, but what she really means is: it would have required me to become a different person, and I'm not sure I would exist in that shape.

Shortcuts become morally suspect. A successful project that didn't require exhaustion feels like a fluke or a fraud. The person who accomplishes it quickly is not respected—she is pitied or suspected. Delegation feels like failure, like an admission that you are not capable, not driven, not worthy. Rest becomes something that happens to other people. Normal people. Lucky people. People whose lives are easier because they are simply less committed.

The feeling goes underground. It lives in the body as muscle tension that doesn't dissolve after a massage, as the constant low vibration of a task list running in the background of consciousness, as the subtle anxiety that surfaces on Sunday evenings and sometimes, if the person is unlucky, never really leaves. It lives as the inability to be surprised by joy. As the assumption that anything good will require payment in exhaustion.

A man in his forties describes his first vacation without work emails in five years. He and his family rented a cottage by the ocean. He sat on a beach. The sun was warm on his shoulders. His children were happy, playing without needing him. And underneath all of this, he felt a gnawing. A sense that something was wrong. That he should be doing something. That this ease was not earned. That it would have to be paid for later, in some form he couldn't yet see. The feeling was not thoughts, exactly. It was a tension in his jaw, a tightness in his throat, a vague sense of dread that wouldn't name itself. So he checked his email anyway. He saw a message from his team. He worked for an hour. Only then could he relax. Only then did the tension in his throat ease. Only then did he feel like he deserved to be there. He didn't realize that his body was requiring him to earn the joy. He thought he was just being responsible.

He is not broken. He is not lazy for wanting to check that email. He is not deficient in his capacity for happiness. He is simply living out the equation. Effort must precede rest. Struggle must validate pleasure. Depletion is the prerequisite for peace. The equation is absolute. It was installed long before he understood what was happening, and it has become so much a part of him that it feels like truth.

* * *

The Jungian shadow does not contain evil. It contains everything that threatens your conscious identity. It holds the disowned parts of yourself—not because they are dark or sinful, but because acknowledging them would shatter the story you have built about who you are.

For people whose identity is fused with effort, the shadow is vast and crowded. It holds the parts of them that know how to rest without guilt. The parts that can ask for help and feel grace instead of shame. The parts that trust life to provide, that play without purpose, that create from desire rather than duty. The parts that are enough without doing anything at all.

These parts are not dark. They are alive. They know about rhythm, about receptivity, about the kind of thinking that happens only in sleep. They know about beauty that serves no function. They know about love that is not earned. They know, at the cellular level, that human beings are not machines. They know that a body at rest is not a body that has failed.

But for the person whose identity is built on effort, these parts are dangerous. They threaten the entire structure. If I can rest and the world doesn't collapse, then what? If I can be loved without exhaustion, if I can be worthy without producing, if I can just be—then who am I? What was all this for? Who have I been all this time?

The conscious self does not want to encounter these questions. So these parts get exiled. They get pushed down, locked away, made unconscious. The person stops noticing them. They become the shadow—not present in consciousness, not available to choice, but active in the background, creating friction, creating the pull toward either rigidity or sudden, inexplicable collapse.

The body knows the shadow is there. The body keeps score. It gets tired in a way that sleep doesn't fix. Eight hours of sleep and the fatigue is still there, a weight in the limbs that no amount of rest can shift. It develops tension that massage releases for only a day, sometimes only an hour. It gets sick at predictable intervals—vacations, promotions, moments when the external structure loosens and there is nothing to push against anymore. The body gets sick as a way of maintaining the equation. If I am resting because I am sick, that is acceptable. The rest is earned through suffering.

The shadow knows something true. It knows that the person is not actually running on discipline or faith. The person is running on the pressure of disowned parts of themselves, pressing against the conscious identity like water against a dam. The energy required to keep those parts suppressed is enormous. The body does the math. Suppression takes more energy than expression. The shadow knows this. It knows that the person is exhausted not because the work is hard, but because the person is working to keep themselves intact, to keep the image of themselves as a hard worker, to keep the shadow pressed down where it can't threaten anything.

One day the dam cracks. The person has a breakdown, a health crisis, an inexplicable depression. The doctor finds nothing wrong, but the person cannot leave the house. The body has made its decision. It has decided that the price of maintaining the identity is now higher than the price of breaking it.

* * *

There is another layer to this, and it is quieter. Deeper. It is the question that lives underneath all of it, the one that rarely reaches words.

If I stop struggling, do I still matter?

This is not an intellectual question. It is a somatic one. It lives in the rib cage as a small terror. It lives in the hands that are always reaching for the next task. It lives in the habit of saying yes to one more thing, and the subtle relief that comes when there is no more time for rest. Because rest means being alone with yourself. Rest means there is no distraction from the question: Am I enough?

For people whose value was installed as effort, this question has never been answered with a yes. They were praised for trying, not for being. They were loved when they were useful, not when they were still. Every moment of safety they received was conditional on performance. So the question has calcified into a belief: I matter only when I am doing something. I matter only when I am needed. I matter only when there is visible evidence of my contribution.

The belief operates like a physical law. It is not subject to argument or evidence. The person could compile a list of moments when they were loved or valued without doing anything, and the belief would remain intact. The mind is very good at maintaining its survival stories.

Stop struggling and you disappear.

Stop struggling and the people who loved you for your usefulness will look away, the way their eyes looked away when the work was done and there was nothing left to show them.

Stop struggling and you become ordinary, which in this equation is the same as invisible.

This is the fear. Not the fear of failure. Not the fear of judgment. But the fear of erasure. The fear that if you stop, you will find out that you were never loved at all—only needed. And need can end. A person can get older, slower, less useful. A person can lose their capacity for effort. And then what? Who will stay?

The body holds this fear as a coiled spring. It keeps the person moving. It makes rest feel impossible, not because of logistics or practical constraints, but because of ontology. Because if I stop, I don't exist.

A woman lies in bed after surgery, unable to work for six weeks. The fear during those weeks is not about recovery or pain. It is about disappearing. Her colleagues continue without her. The company doesn't need her. She is not indispensable. Her mind tries to comfort her with the fact that they're just being professional, but her nervous system hears something else: you were wanted for what you do, not for who you are. Now that you're not doing, now that you're just being, where is the wanting?

The fear is so intense that she goes back to work early. She sits in meetings and her incision aches, but the fear of not mattering is worse than the pain. She has to prove, even from a hospital bed, that she is still useful. That she is still necessary. That she still exists.

* * *

In the space where this fear lives, many people encounter something unexpected: a whisper of ease. A project that somehow gets done with less struggle than they anticipated. A day when their body insists on rest and nothing terrible happens. A person in their life who stays present with them even when they are not achieving anything. A moment when someone looks at them and says, "I love you, not because of what you do, but because you exist."

These moments are small. They are almost imperceptible. But they begin to create a cognitive dissonance. The equation they have been living says one thing. The world is saying something else.

Not everyone hears it. Many people will work harder to reinforce the equation, to prove that it is still true, that ease is still dangerous. They will find new projects, new crises, new reasons why stopping is not an option right now. They will work until they have a heart attack. They will work until their relationships dissolve. They will work until their body gives out in a way that can't be ignored. Then, from the wreckage, they will go back to work.

But some people begin to notice the dissonance. They begin to suspect—very quietly, with a shame they don't yet have words for—that the equation might be wrong. Or at least not as absolute as they thought. A partner tells them, "I like you when you're resting. You're softer. You're here." A therapist asks, "What if your worth is not contingent on what you produce?" A friend stops reaching out to them for advice and asks, instead, "How are you? Not what you've done. How are you?" These moments are small. But they create fissures in the belief system.

There is a woman who has been working at the same intense pace for twenty years when her mother dies. During the funeral arrangements, she cannot work. There are things to do, yes, but they are the things grief requires, not the things productivity requires. She is slow. She makes mistakes. She forgets to return emails. The world does not end. The people who love her do not leave. They draw closer. They bring her soup. They sit with her while she cries. Nothing in the equation prepares her for this.

After the funeral, she goes back to work. But something has shifted. The fear is still there, the habit is still there, but there is also now a question mark. What if they stay anyway? What if I matter even when I'm not doing?

That question mark is the crack. That is where the dissonance lives. That is the threshold.

* * *

You are reading this chapter at a moment when you might be noticing this dissonance yourself. You might be exhausted in a way that sleep doesn't fix. You might be looking at your productivity and seeing not achievement but ashes. You might be wondering, quietly, if there is another way to live that doesn't require you to disappear into your work.

The question that lives underneath everything is still unanswered: If I stop struggling, do I still matter?

You can feel the weight of it in your shoulders right now. You can feel it in the part of you that is relieved, even as you read these words, that you have scheduled something after this, that there is still more to do today, that you are not resting too much.

The answer, when it comes, will not be what the equation taught you to expect. It will not be comfortable. But it will be true. And before we can live into it, we have to see the equation clearly. We have to trace the shape of it in our own lives. We have to watch how it moves in our bodies. We have to feel it in our throats when someone suggests we do less. We have to admit, finally, that the effort has never been about the work. It has always been about the person behind the work. It has always been about proving something that was supposed to have been proven in a kitchen, thirty years ago, with a hand on a shoulder and the whispered promise that trying is enough.

It was never enough. The body has known this all along. And that is the crisis at the heart of everything that follows.

Chapter Three

The Survival Economy

Your chest is tight. Not from anxiety. From carrying weight that isn't yours. You've been carrying it so long you stopped noticing it was weight at all—you thought it was your shape, the way you're made.

It's Tuesday morning and your phone is already warm from messages. Your mother. Your colleague. Your friend who is falling apart again. Your partner who needs you to remember what he forgot. The weight settles in before your feet touch the ground. You open your eyes and the jaw clench is already there, a small stone beneath the skin.

This is not ambition. This is architecture.

Most people don't wake up one day and decide to become the person who holds everything together. It happens in small moments, invisible trades. You do the work that no one else remembers needs doing. You catch the thing before it breaks. You see the shape of what's falling apart and you move toward it instead of away. You get good at it. So good that people forget how to do it without you.

Someone has to notice the kitchen is running low on coffee. Someone has to make sure the deadline gets met, that the email gets sent, that the person who is spiraling gets one kind word before they dissolve. You notice. You act. The family, the workplace, the friend group—it smooths. It works. The gratitude comes in small doses. Not enough to sustain you, but enough to confirm the logic. You are the structure. Without you, shape collapses into chaos.

And then something shifts. You're not the kid anymore who proved love by being useful. You're the adult who earns belonging by being necessary. The machinery of it is the same. Only now money is involved. Paychecks come with the understanding that you are the one who will stay late. Who will solve the unforeseen problem. Who will absorb the emotional labor nobody put in the job description. And exhaustion is not a sign you're working too hard. It's proof that you're working at the frequency that matters.

* * *

There's a difference between being needed and being expressed. Nobody teaches this distinction. It lives in the body before it reaches language.

Being needed is transactional. I will do the thing you cannot do, and in exchange I get to exist in your life. I get a role. You depend on me and that dependence feels like proof. Proof of something. Worth. Purpose. A reason to be here instead of not. The dependency is the evidence. The mechanism of validation.

The problem with being needed is that it requires someone else's lack. Your value is their inability. If they got better, learned, remembered, organized themselves—your purpose deflates. So there's a strange economy at work in most over-functioning relationships. Not conscious. Not intentional. But there. A woman overheard in a coffee shop, speaking to her therapist: "If I stop managing him, he'll fall apart. And if he falls apart, I'm basically responsible. I'm the thing holding him up." The therapist asked what would happen if that were true. Long silence. She finally said: "Then I matter." The survival economy speaks in that silence.

Being expressed is different. It's generative, not transactional. I show up with what I have because I have it, not because you lack it. You could do the thing without me. The work I do doesn't need your incapacity to exist. When you get better, my work doesn't evaporate. We just have different work now. This is almost unimaginable to someone trained in the survival economy. How can you matter if your effort isn't essential? How can you belong if you're not irreplaceable?

Most people have never been raised to be expressed. They've been trained—sometimes gently, sometimes not—to be needed. The subtle message arrives in a thousand variations. *You're such a helper. We don't know what we'd do without you. You're the only one we can count on. You always know what to do.* These feel like praise. They function as assignment. A child hears them and learns to check the room for what's needed. Learns to scan. Learns that her own internal state is secondary information compared to the temperature of everyone else's emotional weather.

By the time you're an adult applying for jobs, the architecture is locked in. You gravitate toward roles where your value lives in your ability to hold things that are falling. You're hired because you solve problems. Because you can manage chaos. Because you don't complain. Because you will take on more than is reasonable and make it look reasonable. Your resume reads like a catalog of crises averted. You got hired three times because you were the only one calm enough to handle the impossible deadline, the impossible client, the impossible project that everyone else had written off.

And the workplace rewards you for this. In money. In title. In the particular kind of recognition that comes from being indispensable. Your manager leans back and says, "I don't know what I'd do without you." And you feel something settle. The contract gets reinforced. The economy expands.

* * *

The work that pays is often the work that costs the most.

This is not metaphorical. There is a literal price. Your nervous system learns to live in a state of low-grade alert. You develop a sixth sense for an incoming problem before anyone else sees it. Your shoulders spend so much time near your ears that the muscle fibers have to be reminded where neutral is. You sleep poorly because you're solving problems in the dark, your unconscious mind still on the clock even when your body is supposed to rest. You eat fast, at your desk, while typing emails, half-chewed food and information processing at the same time. You get sick sometimes, in that particular way where your body finally demands you stop—not because you're weak, but because there's a finite amount of fuel and you've been burning through it on a timeframe that was never sustainable. A man in an office bathroom, shoulders hunched over the sink, splashing water on his face at 11 PM on a Tuesday, thinking about the report due Wednesday and the client conversation Thursday and his daughter's soccer game Saturday that he'll probably skip again.

But there's also a psychological price. A relational one.

When your identity is constructed around holding things together, you become the person who cannot fall apart. You are the competence in the room. The steady one. The person who has it handled. Which means you cannot ask for help. Cannot admit confusion. Cannot say *I don't know what I'm doing*. Because that collapses the whole structure. It collapses your job, your identity, your proof of belonging. You have to know. You have to have figured it out. You have to be the one with answers while others are drowning in questions.

You learn to manage everything alone, or with the particular efficiency of someone who doesn't have time to be vulnerable. You become a problem-solver before you become a person. You achieve before you rest. You give more than you have because if you only gave what you had, it might not be enough. Your internal resource is treated as a well you haven't found the bottom of yet. You keep drawing. Eventually there are days when you pull the bucket up and it comes back nearly empty. But you don't rest. You just pull harder.

And somewhere in this, connection gets replaced with utility. The people in your life don't know you because you're too busy being useful to be known. They know your competence. Your availability. Your ability to remember what they forgot and hold what they dropped. They know you're the one who will take their catastrophe and turn it into a thing they can live with. But they don't know the you underneath that architecture. Because there's no time to build it. And because showing it might require someone else to step up, and you're not sure they can handle that weight. What if you need help and no one knows how to give it because you never learned to receive it?

So you stay behind the role. Professional. Reliable. Necessary. You become excellent at absence. The absence of complaint. The absence of need. The absence of self that might inconvenience someone else.

* * *

There is a reason this feels like survival.

In families where one child becomes the holder—the one who notices when mom is overwhelmed and gets very quiet so as not to add to it, the one who manages their parent's emotions and adjusts their own needs accordingly—this is not character development. This is a strategy. A child observes that their parents have limits. That the family can become unstable. That there's a fragility beneath the adult surface. And they move toward responsibility not out of virtue, but out of fear. If I'm the one holding things together, at least I'm not falling. At least I know what happens next. At least I have some control in a situation where control otherwise feels impossible.

It's not a choice. It's an adaptation. A brilliant, creative, necessary adaptation to an unsafe situation. The nervous system recalibrates. The child's antennae get sharper. By age eight, she can walk into a room and know her mother's mood from the particular way she's loading the dishwasher. By age ten, she anticipates requests before they're made. She becomes the one who remembers what everyone needs because remembering is the thing that makes her invisible, and invisibility in that house means safety.

And adaptations are smart. They work. They're survival strategies that genuinely save lives, stabilize families, prevent collapses. They are evidence of intelligence, resilience, and an extraordinary capacity to read a room and move with precision inside it. Until they don't work anymore. Until you're forty years old and the weight is so old and so heavy that you can't distinguish it from yourself anymore. Until being needed feels so much like being loved that you don't know how to exist without it. Until the architecture becomes the prison it was designed to escape.

The survival economy runs on this fuel: *I will give more than I have, and in return I will be allowed to stay.*

It's a contract you never signed. It was never verbalized. You certainly never agreed to it consciously. But you've been keeping it for years. Decades maybe. And the cost has become the architecture of your life. The fine print was written in your body language. The signatures are in every choice you've made. The payment plan extends into your future in ways you're only beginning to understand.

You know how to run on empty because you learned early that there was no other option. You know how to absorb chaos—a chaotic parent, a chaotic workplace, a chaotic relationship—and convert it into something functional, something bearable. You are a transformer of disorder. You take the noise and the fragmentation and you build a structure inside it. You know how to be less so that someone else can be more. You know how to occupy the smallest space in the room while somehow keeping all the pieces from scattering. You do this so well that people barely notice you're doing it at all. They just experience their world becoming more manageable.

And the body knows all of this. The body keeps the contract even when the mind has stopped believing in it. Your nervous system tightens at the thought of someone else being in trouble. Your attention splits between what you're doing and what they might need. You cannot rest completely because rest feels like abandonment. Like breaking the deal. Like betrayal of the original agreement, the one made in silence all those years ago: *I will be indispensable, and you will keep me.*

* * *

The cost compounds in ways that are hard to measure.

There's the cost to creativity. Most of the people stuck in survival economies are people with a lot to say, a lot to make, a lot to offer the world that has nothing to do with managing other people's crises. But that part gets postponed. Because the urgent work—the work that proves you belong—always comes first. And the urgent work is never finished. A woman in a writing group says quietly: "I always have ideas right before bed. By morning they're gone because I spent the night listening to my partner's work drama, and by morning I'm already tired." The urgent eats everything. The creative dies not from lack of ability but from chronic triage. You never get to the thing that's yours.

There's the cost to your actual relationships. The people you love don't know you because you're not present to them—you're present to their needs. You're solving. You're managing. You're three steps ahead, trying to prevent the thing you fear. Real intimacy requires being seen, and being seen requires being willing to be small, confused, not-okay sometimes. The survival economy doesn't allow for this. So you have people around you and you're lonely. You're the one everyone comes to, and you're the one no one really knows. Your best friends have never heard you say you're struggling because struggling is something that happens to other people, and you're the person who helps those people get stable again.

There's the cost to your health. This is the one that eventually breaks through denial. The body gets tired. It gets angry. It forgets how to regulate itself because it's been in sympathetic activation for so long. Chronic pain blooms in your shoulders and neck. Insomnia becomes not occasional but your actual sleep architecture. Autoimmune issues emerge—the body turning inward when it has nowhere else to go. Digestive problems. Headaches that arrive like clock work. Hair loss. Skin that won't heal. These are not separate from the survival economy—they're the economy's bill, finally coming due. The body was never meant to run at this frequency. It tries to send messages. Most people ignore them and just take another pill.

And there's the cost to your capacity to know what you actually want. When your entire operating system is built around knowing what other people need, your own desires become opaque. You don't know what you like because you haven't practiced liking anything. You only know what you should do, what they need, what will keep the machine running. When someone asks what you want, there's a blank. A real one. Not false modesty. An actual absence. You've spent so long tracking everyone else's internal weather that your own has become background noise.

* * *

Burnout is not a failure of stamina.

This is important. It's the difference between being broken and being accurate. Burnout is not what happens when you're not strong enough to keep going. It's what happens when you keep going anyway. It's the body's honest report about a situation that was never sustainable. It's the nervous system finally saying no when the mind won't. It's depletion speaking the truth the will refuses to hear.

A person running a survival economy for ten, fifteen, twenty years—this person is not failing at sustainability. They're succeeding at something that was never meant to be sustained. They're performing a feat of endurance that should have been impossible. The fact that it eventually breaks isn't weakness. It's accuracy.

The architecture was an emergency measure. Emergency measures have a window. They work for crises. A week without sleep when someone is dying—you can do that. A month of extra hours to save a company—you can do that. But you can't do a decade. The human system doesn't have that capacity. And yet most people in survival economies never get the signal until it's too late. They just get more tired. They interpret the exhaustion as a personal failing—not disciplined enough, not resilient enough, not good enough at managing their time, not determined enough. They push harder. And the pushing is what finally cracks things open.

Sometimes a relationship ends because the other person finally realized they were talking to a function, not a person. They met resistance for the first time. The steady giver suddenly couldn't give. And instead of understanding that the structure had collapsed because it was never sustainable, they felt abandoned. The person who had given everything had nothing left, and it felt like betrayal. Both people left confused about what happened.

Sometimes work collapses because the one person who was holding it all has nothing left to give. The project fails. The clients leave. Everyone looks at you, shocked, because you were the one who always had it handled. They didn't know you were running on fumes. They didn't know the machine was held together by your will alone.

Sometimes the body just stops working in a way that can't be ignored. The illness is real. The pain is real. The exhaustion is so complete that even the guilt about resting can't override it anymore. The body makes the choice the mind never would.

This is not failure. This is information.

* * *

There's something specific that happens when you start to see the architecture for what it is.

At first it feels terrible. Because for so long, this survival economy has felt like your identity. Like the thing that makes you valuable. Like the thing that proves you're not lazy, not selfish, not a burden. And if you stop keeping the contract—if you give less than you have, if you let someone else figure out their own crisis, if you admit you don't know what happens next—then what are you?

The fear is real. The fear is ancient. It's the fear of a small person who learned that their safety depended on being useful. It's the fear that you'll be abandoned the moment you become inconvenient. That you'll discover you were only tolerated, never actually wanted. And that fear doesn't just disappear because you're an adult now and understand it logically. The nervous system doesn't care about logic. It remembers the original stakes.

But something else becomes visible too. The weight. Not metaphorically. The actual weight of it. You start to notice that your neck hurts. That your jaw is clenched even when you're supposedly relaxing. That you cannot sit through a dinner with friends without your phone in your hand, ready to manage someone else's emergency. That you make decisions based on what will cause the least disturbance to other people, not on what you actually want. That the last time you made a choice purely because it pleased you, you can't remember.

You see the cost more clearly than you ever have. Not in a way that leads to self-blame—that would be the old pattern, turning this awareness into another reason to try harder, another failure to metabolize into fuel. But in a way that leads to something like grief. Grief for all the time spent managing. All the creativity that got postponed. All the relationships that never got to be real because you were too busy being needed. All the versions of yourself that didn't get built because the blueprint was always about serving the structure, never about becoming yourself.

And underneath the grief, if you let it be there, is something else. Something that looks like the beginning of a choice.

Because you're not seven years old anymore. You're not actually going to be abandoned if you're not useful. People don't actually need you the way they used to. Some of them think they do. Some will insist they do. But they're confusing what they want with what they need. And that's their work to figure out, not yours to solve. You're not responsible for their relationship to your limits. You're not in charge of managing their disappointment.

The survival economy gave you something. It gave you a role when you didn't know who you were. It gave you a way to belong when belonging felt conditional. It kept you focused on something outside yourself when the inside felt unsafe. It worked. It genuinely did. You're alive because of it. The family didn't dissolve. The crisis got managed. You mattered.

But you're not that small anymore. And the contract—the one that was never written down, never agreed to, never renegotiated—is finally up for revision.

Not because you have to be selfish now. Not because you have to stop caring about people. Not because the answer is to do nothing and let everything fall apart. Those would be different prisons, just arranged differently.

But because there's another way to exist in the world. One where you don't have to give more than you have. One where being you is enough without the doing attached to it. One where people might actually stay because they like you, not because you're useful to them. One where rest is not abandonment. One where your needs matter too.

It's hard to imagine. It was never modeled. The nervous system has no template for it. But it's possible. It's starting to become visible. Like a shape emerging from fog. Not clear yet. Not certain. But there.

The weight is still there. You can feel it. It hasn't lifted. But now you know it's weight. And knowing is where everything begins to shift.

Chapter Four

Why the Nervous System Distrusts Ease

The first time ease felt wrong, you probably didn't notice it was happening.

You'd put down the task. Stepped back from the screen. Sent the email that had been sitting, half-written, in your chest for three days. And then—a strange sensation bloomed in the space where the urgency had been. Not relief. Relief comes after effort, and it comes with the body saying yes, we can rest now. This was different. This was your body saying nothing, and the silence felt dangerous.

Your hand found your phone. Your mind returned to the list of things you should be doing. Not because they were actually urgent. But because the absence of something—that hum, that electric readiness—felt like standing on a platform with nothing beneath it. Your attention kept snagging on small failures. That typo in the email you'd already sent. The task you hadn't completed yet. The person you meant to follow up with last week. The quality of attention shifted. What had been a moment of completion became a moment of scanning.

This is what a nervous system sounds like when it doesn't trust peace.

* * *

For years, your body has been living in a particular architecture of sensation. Tension in the shoulders. A certain rhythm to your breathing—quick, shallow, ready. The particular chemical signature of cortisol and adrenaline, which your system has learned to interpret as proof that you are managing, handling, staying ahead. These aren't comfortable sensations. But they are *known*. They have maps. Your nervous system can move through them the way you move through a room you've lived in for twenty years—automatically, without thought, just the familiar muscles engaging in the familiar pattern.

Listen to someone who has been in this state. Not them describing it, but them living it: they're speaking quickly, their words tumbling over each other. They interrupt themselves. Their hand is moving even when they're sitting still. There's a brightness in their eyes that looks like energy but is really activation. They look engaged. They look like they care. They look—and this is the insidious part—like they are working. And for people whose identity has been built on the evidence of work, this visible activation becomes proof of worth.

Ease dissolves that architecture. The shoulders drop. The breathing lengthens. The hand stills. The words slow. And in that dissolution, something primal in the nervous system reads danger.

This is not laziness. This is not lack of discipline. This is not even—as it often feels—weakness. This is basic neurobiology. The nervous system's primary job is prediction. It reads the environment and attempts to forecast what comes next so that the body can prepare. When the environment contains a constant hum of threat—whether that threat is real or internalized—the nervous system becomes expert at that particular frequency. It tunes itself to it. It expects it. It requires it.

When the threat disappears, prediction becomes impossible.

The absence of tension is not the absence of threat. It is the absence of data. Without the familiar signals of effort, without the body's practiced postures and chemical certainties, the nervous system cannot forecast what is coming next. And when you cannot forecast, you cannot prepare. And when you cannot prepare, you are vulnerable. Or so the system believes. Or so it has been taught.

So it does what it has always done. It scans harder. It listens for the thing that must be coming. It dredges up a new task, a new worry, a new incompleteness. The scanning is not optional. It is the system doing its job. It is the system being responsible, in the only way it knows how.

This is why ease so often feels like the moment before something goes wrong.

The body has learned that calm is prelude. That rest is the interval between catastrophes. That the only reliable state is the state of bracing.

* * *

There is a particular kind of person who remembers the exact texture of struggle the way other people remember their mother's voice.

A woman sits at her kitchen table, coffee going cold. She's just finished a three-hour work session—the kind where she enters at nine and surfaces at noon, startled to find the morning gone. The work is done. She knows it's done. She has done this enough times to recognize the feeling of completion. And yet her fingers are still moving toward her laptop. Her attention is still half-turned toward the next thing. When she finally forces herself to close the computer, she experiences something like vertigo. The day stretches in front of her. Empty hours. She feels briefly, acutely, like a person with no purpose.

Another version: a man in a meeting. He has solved the problem they were discussing. The solution came to him while he was listening to someone else talk—a kind of mental ease, a kind of drift that allowed the answer to surface. He starts to relax. And then his body tightens. He begins to poke holes in his own solution. He lists objections that only he has raised. He makes the problem harder again, because a harder problem requires his attention, his effort, his proof that he is necessary.

Neither of these people is broken. They have simply spent so long in effort that they have lost the grammar of anything else. Tension speaks clearly. Effort has structure. Struggle has a beginning, a middle, an end. The body knows exactly what to do when there is a deadline, when someone is depending on them, when the stakes are visible and real and pressing. The breathing quickens in a way that makes sense. The muscles tighten in specific locations that correspond to specific tasks. The mind narrows in a way that feels like focus, like purpose, like proof that the effort is justified because look at how hard we are working.

Even when this effort yields nothing. Even when the tension produces only more tension, the spiral familiar enough now that it passes for stability. The person knows how to be in struggle. They do not know how to be in anything else.

Ease requires a completely different physiology. Not the opposite of tension—not a dead weight, not a collapse into exhaustion. But something else entirely. A breathing pattern that has never been practiced. A hormonal signature that the body does not recognize as safe because it does not recognize it as anything. A state in which the muscles can soften without the person disappearing. In which the mind can widen without the task falling apart. In which productivity does not require suffering.

Most people have never felt this while working. They have felt it in the hours before sleep, in the moment after sex, in rare afternoons when nothing was required and nobody was watching. But never while doing something that mattered. Never while creating something that someone might judge. Never while the world was watching. Never while something was actually at stake.

So when ease arrives—actually arrives, not as a fantasy but as a real state in the body—the nervous system responds with genuine confusion. Is this a trap? Is this the moment of vulnerability before the attack? Is this the softening that only happens right before the fall? The body does not have a category for doing good work while feeling good. It is a category that has never existed in the architecture of this nervous system.

So it begins to construct one, frantically, pulling from every memory of ease before disaster. The calm before the layoff. The peace before the diagnosis. The ease in the relationship before the betrayal. The body is searching its archives for every time it dropped its guard and then paid for it.

* * *

This is when guilt appears.

Guilt has been misnamed for a very long time. We have been taught to believe that guilt is a moral emotion—the voice of conscience, the sign that we have done something wrong. And guilt certainly wears that costume. It says things like "I should still be working. I should still be worried. I don't deserve this ease. Something is wrong with me for feeling okay. I'm being irresponsible. I'm shortchanging the people who depend on me."

The voice is so specific. It is so certain. It sounds exactly like wisdom, like the internalized voice of every person who ever taught you that worth was something that had to be earned through exhaustion.

But the voice speaking those words is not your morality. It is your nervous system.

Guilt, in this context, is a regulatory signal. It is the body's way of saying that a familiar pattern has been interrupted, and it needs that pattern restored in order to continue functioning. Guilt produces tension. Tension produces the chemical signatures—the cortisol, the adrenaline, the slight tightness in the throat—that the nervous system has learned to interpret as safety. And suddenly, once again, the body can predict what comes next. It can organize itself. It can move.

The guilt is not telling you that you did something wrong. It is saying something changed and I don't know how to organize myself in response. It is a somatic distress signal masquerading as moral wisdom.

You can test this. The next time you experience guilt in the aftermath of ease—the moment when you've stopped overworking and some part of you insists you should feel worse—pay attention to what happens in your body. Notice where the guilt lives. It is not in your conscience. It is not in some abstract sense of right and wrong. It is in your chest. In the tightening across your shoulders. In your jaw. In the way your breathing becomes shallow again. It is the reconstruction of tension. It is the nervous system re-establishing the conditions under which it knows how to function.

This is why the guilt never comes with a list of specific things you've done wrong. It is free-floating, sourceless, a quality of emotional weather rather than a response to an action. It does not say "you should feel guilty because you forgot to call your mother." It simply says "something is wrong" without specifying what. That vagueness is the tell. That undirected quality is proof that something else is happening beneath the moral language.

Pay attention to the moment when you notice this. The moment when you see that the guilt is not responding to your actions but to your physiology. The moment when you realize that your nervousness system is not lecturing you about morality but attempting to restore a pattern. Once you see this, you cannot unsee it. The guilt is not a character flaw. It is a somatic event being translated into moral language. And that translation is a choice, not an inevitability.

* * *

The language of "cheating" reveals the same translation mechanism.

People use this word constantly. A writer uses an AI tool to draft a section and a voice appears: "Isn't that cheating?" Someone delegates a task they thought they had to do themselves and the question blooms unbidden. Another person discovers a shortcut that cuts their work in half and the accusation lands like a verdict: "You're taking the easy way out."

The voice is so insistent. It is so certain that there is something morally wrong with taking the easier path. It rings with the authority of every teacher who marked your work down for using a calculator. Every parent who implied that you hadn't really earned your success if it came too easily. Every culture that equates struggle with virtue and ease with laziness or moral compromise.

But listen to that voice not as a judge but as a body. Listen to what it is actually saying beneath the ethical language.

What the nervous system is saying is: this is not the architecture I know. This is not the pattern I have learned to predict within. This is a different rhythm, a different posture, a different chemical state. This is unfamiliar. And unfamiliar is threat. There is no map in my system for this territory.

A woman sits down to write. For fifteen years, she has written by hand, slowly, laboriously, generating each sentence through friction and effort. Then she tries dictating. The words come faster. She says them aloud and they are already shaped, already revised, already moving at the speed of thought. She can feel the difference in her body. There is less tension in her shoulders. Her breathing is easier. And something in her seizes. She feels like a fraud. Like she is not really writing anymore, just... talking. Speaking instead of creating. The moral language—that this is somehow less legitimate—arrives almost instantly. But what she is actually experiencing is discontinuity. The mismatch between the old pattern and the new one.

The moral language is a translation. It is the nervous system taking a somatic experience of discontinuity and rendering it as an ethical problem. Because ethical problems are easier to work with than the rawer truth: your nervous system is terrified because it has lost its map. It is disoriented. It cannot predict what comes next.

The reframe is crucial because it changes what you can do about it. If cheating is a moral failure, then you must choose between your integrity and your ease. You must suffer to be good. You must earn rest through exhaustion. This is the original deal, the one that has cost you decades. This is the architecture that has built you and unmade you.

But if cheating is a somatic event—if it is simply the nervous system's alarm at encountering a state it has never learned to tolerate—then it is not a choice you are making. It is a sensation you are having. It is information, not verdict. And sensations can change. Nervous systems can learn. The architecture can be rebuilt.

* * *

The body keeps score not of morality but of pattern.

Someone who has spent twenty years organizing their identity around effort will have a nervous system that is exquisitely tuned to effort's signature. Every molecule of their being has learned the shape of that particular struggle. The breathing has become automatic—shallow, quick, from the top of the lungs. The tightness in the shoulders has become so familiar it feels like a neutral state, like how their body is supposed to be. The anxiety has become invisible, woven so thoroughly into the baseline that they do not notice it anymore. It is just the color of their consciousness. It is just how it feels to be alive.

Then something shifts. Small at first. They use a tool that cuts the task in half. They delegate something they thought they had to do themselves. They take a day off and something still gets done. They work on a project that actually aligns with their skills and their interests and they enter that state of flow where time moves differently. And suddenly they are not organizing anymore through force. Suddenly they are just living.

The nervous system reads this as catastrophic discontinuity.

And the body does what it does with discontinuity. It screams. Not metaphorically. Literally. The nervous system generates feelings of guilt, shame, anxiety, unworthiness—all of these are somatic events, all of them have a location in the body, all of them serve the same function: they reestablish the familiar pattern. They bring back the tension. They restore the chemical state that the body recognizes as home, even though home has been exhausting.

A man stops his brutal morning routine—the four a.m. wake-up, the two-hour workout, the constant optimization. He is tired. He experiments with waking at six, with a gentler practice, with allowing his body to rest. The work is actually better. His thinking is clearer. His creativity is sharper. And he is wracked with guilt. Something must be wrong. He is being lazy. He is compromising his standards. He is letting himself go. The language arrives with such force that it drowns out the evidence of his own experience. And often, this guilt is sufficient. It pulls him back into the familiar architecture. He sets the alarm for four a.m. again. The punishment resumes. The body settles.

This is not weakness. This is not failure. This is the nervous system doing exactly what it was designed to do: predict the future, forecast threat, attempt to maintain the conditions under which survival is possible.

The tragedy is that the nervous system is working with outdated information. It is predicting based on the world that created it—the world in which effort really was the only way to prove worth, in which struggle really was the price of belonging, in which the only safe way to move through life was to move quickly, move tensely, move in a state of constant readiness. The world in which rest was a luxury and productivity was a moral virtue and the only way to be safe was to never, ever stop.

That world still exists. It still exists for many of the people you know. But it does not have to be your world anymore. And the nervous system cannot learn this until the body has proof. Until the nervous system can practice ease long enough to learn that ease is not the prelude to disaster. That ease is not a trap. That ease is not the moment you let your guard down and lose everything.

* * *

The somatic invitation, then, is this: what does ease actually feel like in the body when it is not filtered through threat?

Most people cannot answer this question. They have been living inside the threat filter so long that they have no idea what the original sensation is. They cannot distinguish between the sensation itself and the alarm system layered over it. It is like trying to describe a color that has been filtered through red glass—you see the color, but you see it through the filter, and you cannot remember anymore what it looks like without the distortion.

You might describe ease as the absence of something—not tense, not anxious, not striving. But that is describing it through negation, which is what the nervous system does when it encounters something unfamiliar. It is like describing blue to someone who has only ever seen gray. It captures something, but it misses the thing itself.

Ease, when it is not filtered through the nervous system's alarm system, is actually something. It is a presence, not an absence.

There is a quality of spaciousness. Not spaciousness in the metaphorical sense—not some abstract sense of having room for possibilities. But actual physical space. A sense in the chest that there is more room to breathe than before. A kind of expansion that happens not through effort but through the removal of constriction. The body being allowed to take up the space it actually occupies, without apology, without the constant tightening that says "smaller, quieter, less." You notice it when you exhale and the shoulders actually drop instead of rising again immediately in anticipation of the next demand.

There is a quality to the exhale. When you have been breathing shallowly for twenty years—breathing with just the top of the lungs, breathing with the shoulders, breathing in a way that matches the constant state of readiness—then a full exhale is not something you can manufacture. It only comes when the threat signal is genuinely gone. And when it comes, it is not a dramatic sigh of relief. It is slower. Longer. The kind of exhale that takes time. The kind that has a rhythm to it, like gravity is actually working with you instead of against you.

There is a softening. Not in the sense of weakness, not in the sense of becoming less capable or less present. But in the jaw. In the space between the eyebrows. In the skin around the eyes. In the small muscles at the base of the skull. These are places where the body holds the constant vigilance, where it braces against the next demand. These are the places that have been clenched so long they have forgotten that unclenching is possible. When they do, it is not comfortable at first. It is unfamiliar. It is strange, almost, to realize how much energy has been spent holding these particular muscles tight. It is like learning to live in a body you have never inhabited before.

There is a quality of groundedness that is different from the groundedness of effort. When you are working hard, when you are pushing, there is a kind of grounding that comes from the body being locked against something—against time, against your own sense of inadequacy, against the weight of other people's expectations. It is the grounding of resistance. This is a different grounding. It is the simple reality of a body sitting in a chair. Of weight settling into a surface. Of gravity being something that holds instead of something you hold against. It is passive, in the way that the earth is passive, and that passivity is revolutionary.

And there is something else. Something harder to name. A kind of simplicity. The noise quiets. Not the noise around you—that may not change. The traffic may still be there. The notifications may still be pinging. The demands may still be waiting. But the constant internal commentary, the way the mind is always running a calculation about whether you are doing enough, whether you are enough, whether this moment is wasted or productive or justified—that quiets.

And in that quiet, there is just the present moment. Just the work, or the rest, or the simple fact of being alive. Just the breath moving in and out of the body.

Most readers will not have vocabulary for this. Not because it is ineffable. But because you have never been in this state while working, and you have never been in this state long enough for language to emerge around it. Your words for calm are words that come from non-working time. They are rested words, vacation words, words for the margins, for the stolen moments. But this ease is different.

This ease happens while you are doing something that matters. This ease coexists with purpose. This ease is not the opposite of productivity—it is productivity without the cost. And you need permission to notice it. You need permission to stop translating it through the nervous system's alarm language. Permission to not call it cheating, or laziness, or unsustainable. Permission to not call it anything but what it is: a different way of organizing yourself in time, in effort, in the whole long project of becoming someone whose work reflects who they actually are.

* * *

Your nervous system will resist this translation for a long time. Years, probably. The guilt will return. The shame about efficiency will bloom without warning. The old language will reappear, dressed in new clothes, insisting that surely, certainly, you must be doing something wrong. You will be in a moment of ease and some part of you will insist that you are missing something, that you are not paying attention to something that matters, that the ease itself is a form of negligence.

And each time, you will have the choice: you can listen to it as a moral voice. You can allow the nervous system's confusion to reestablish the old architecture of tension. You can step back into struggle because it is familiar and because at least in struggle you know who you are.

Or you can notice it as what it is. A signal that something has changed. That your body is attempting to maintain a pattern that no longer serves you. That somewhere in the silence of ease, your nervous system is scanning for the threat that used to be there. That somewhere in the comfort, your body is searching for the fight that used to define it.

It is not your enemy. It is not your saboteur. It is not even a flaw in your design. It is your body, trying to keep you safe in the only way it knows how. It is your nervous system, doing its job with the information it has. What it does not yet understand is that the danger has already passed. The world that demanded struggle as the price of survival has already ended, at least for you, at least right now.

The exhale is not the moment before something goes wrong. It is the moment after something goes right. It is not the absence of protection but the presence of something else entirely. Something that your body is learning, slowly, to trust.

That learning takes time. That learning takes repetition. That learning asks you to notice, again and again, that ease did not destroy you. That ease was not a trap. That ease was real.

PART II

WHAT VALUE ACTUALLY IS

Chapter Five

Orientation Is the New Value

The woman across from me had been crying for three minutes straight, the kind of cry that comes after months of holding. Not the loud kind. The kind where your shoulders shake and you can't quite catch your breath and you feel like you're drowning in a room full of air.

I didn't tell her to stop.

I didn't offer her tissues or reassurance or any of the small deflections we use to manage someone else's grief. I just sat there. The room held her crying the way water holds weight. And then, when the shaking slowed—not stopped, just slowed—I said something simple: "You've been running on fumes for so long that rest feels like falling."

She stopped. Not from shock or correction, but from recognition. Her body stilled. The tension in her jaw released first, then her shoulders dropped perhaps an inch. She looked at me and said, "Yes. Exactly that."

Nothing had changed in her circumstance. No problem had been solved. No insight had been delivered like a gift wrapped and handed over. No action plan emerged. And yet something had shifted. The quality of her presence in the room was different. She wasn't alone with the unnamed thing anymore. It had a shape now. It had words. Her experience had moved from something happening *to* her—a malfunction, a failure to cope—into something she could see. Something she could stand beside instead of being buried under.

This is what orientation does.

* * *

We live in an age of information glut. You can find the answer to almost anything in seconds. How to cook an egg. How to fix a relationship. How to manage anxiety. The data is there, infinite and indexed and available at three in the morning when you can't sleep and your mind is racing through forty possible next moves. There are newsletters about sleep optimization. TikToks about nervous system regulation. Podcasts explaining the neurochemistry of procrastination. Entire industries built on the premise that if you just had the right information, you would finally get it right.

And yet people are more lost than ever.

Not lost in the sense of lacking information. Lost in the sense of not knowing where they stand. Lost in the sense of having climbed so high that they can't see the ground anymore and can't remember why they started climbing. Lost in the sense of standing in front of your own life and feeling like you're looking at someone else's blueprint.

A client sent me a message once: "I have all the tools. Why do I still feel like I'm missing something?"

The missing thing wasn't a tool. It wasn't another framework or system or morning routine. It was a map. It was someone saying, "Here. You are here. This is what that feels like. This is what it means. This is not a problem you need to solve. This is information your body is sending you."

Information says: Do this. Follow these steps in this order. You'll get a result.

Orientation says: This is where you stand right now. This is the shape of where you've been. This is what your body is telling you right now. This is what it's like to be you at this moment.

One is about knowledge transfer. One is about clarity. One comes from outside. The other arrives when someone who sees clearly points it out to you. The difference is the difference between a recipe and a cook standing beside you saying,

"Feel the dough. When it starts sticking to your hands like this, you're close. Don't fight it. Let it show you what it needs."

* * *

There's a phenomenon I notice in people who've spent years in the effort economy. They have the survival skills of small gods. They can manage three crises simultaneously while their own nervous system screams. They can sense what others need before those people know it themselves. They can absorb criticism and extract the useful part while letting the rest run off like water. Their skin has thickened in the places where it matters most. They've become expert at translation, at reading subtext, at knowing exactly what pitch of voice will calm someone down or spur them forward. They know how to hold the room and how to disappear into it.

What they cannot do is sit still without panic.

What they cannot do is trust that something important might be happening in the space where nothing is being produced. That something real is occurring in the silence. That their body knows things their mind hasn't caught up to yet. That rest is not a failure of discipline but an instruction.

A woman I worked with called it "the static." She sat with me one afternoon, her hands moving in small agitated circles, her leg bouncing a rhythm that seemed to belong to someone else's body, and said, "When I'm not doing anything, there's just this white noise. And I can't tell if something's wrong or if I'm just finally hearing what was always there."

I asked her to describe the static. What did it feel like. Where in her body did she feel it. When did it start.

She put her hand on her chest. Her fingers splayed across the center, pressing down as if to anchor herself. "It's like... electricity. Like my whole system is still running but there's nowhere to go. It's building up behind my eyes. It wants to move but I'm telling it not to. It's like my body's stuck in the on position and I've forgotten how to turn it off."

The static was her body. It was the sound of her nervous system trying to calibrate back down from high alert. It was the sensation of muscles that had been clenched for fifteen years finally getting the signal that it was safe to release. It was the sensation of being alive in a way she'd learned not to trust. It was confusion and grief and the strange lightness that comes when you stop carrying weight you didn't know you were carrying. It was her own aliveness becoming visible to her, and it terrified her because it looked like failure.

When I named it—not as a problem, not as something that needed fixing, not as a symptom requiring treatment, but as information—the quality of her relationship to it changed. She could feel it without fighting it. She could be curious about it instead of terrified by it. She stopped asking "What's wrong with me?" and started asking "What is my body trying to tell me?" The static became something she was experiencing rather than something that was happening to her, something that proved she was broken. It became data instead of diagnosis.

The name was the thing that made the difference. Not because naming it fixed it. But because naming it moved it from *happening-to-me* to *happening-in-me*. From invasion to information. From pathology to process. From something that meant she was failing to something that meant she was arriving. The static became her nervous system speaking in the only language it had learned—urgency, motion, the belief that if she stopped moving, everything would collapse.

* * *

I think about the difference between being told something and being shown something.

You can tell someone, "You've based your worth on your productivity, and that's connected to your childhood experience of conditional love." That's true. That's useful. That's information. You can see them nod. They know this is true in the way you know something intellectually. It lands in the thinking mind and sits there like a fact. A fact about themselves that proves they're broken, that they have this defect, this architecture of damage.

Or you can sit with that person and watch the exact moment their face changes when they realize—not think, but *feel*—that the way they talk to themselves when they rest is the way their parent talked to them when they weren't performing. Watch them watch themselves being ungentle. Watch their shoulders cave slightly as they see it. Watch that recognition land in their body the way a stone lands in still water, creating ripples outward. Watch them realize it's not a character flaw. It's a learned behavior. It's something their nervous system was trained to do, back when doing something was the only way to matter.

That's not information. That's a mirror. That's orientation.

The mirror doesn't come from having the right words. It comes from having seen the same territory so many times that you can recognize it in someone else's face. It comes from having walked through that territory yourself. It comes from having tracked your own confusion long enough to know its shape and smell and color. It comes from paying attention. From watching. From allowing yourself to notice what you're noticing instead of moving away from it.

A man once told me about his therapist: "She said something small about how I was talking about my body like it was a problem I had to solve. And I just... knew that was true. Not because it was a revelation, but because I'd already felt it. She was just confirming something I already knew. But I needed someone else to say it before I could trust that I wasn't crazy. Like, I'd been experiencing this the whole time but I couldn't trust my own perception of it until someone else named it. And then suddenly it was real. It was real because she saw it too."

Language isn't decorative. It's not optional. It's not merely a nice addition to clarity. It's structural. It holds things in place. It builds meaning. It makes the invisible visible. It transforms private experience into shared reality. When someone who is not you speaks the truth you've been living but couldn't quite claim, it changes the architecture of your understanding. The thing you've been carrying alone suddenly has witnesses. It becomes real in a different way. You can point to it. You can say it. You can stop being the only person who knows it's happening. The shame moves slightly. There's now someone standing with you in it.

* * *

There's something curious happening in the culture right now.

We have more teachers than ever. More content. More courses. More access to expertise and methodology and step-by-step systems. A person can spend their entire life consuming resources about how to live better and still feel fundamentally unguided. Still feel like they're floating. Still feel like everyone else has the map and they're just pretending.

Because information and guidance are not the same thing. They're not even on the same spectrum.

Information is declarative: "Here's what this means. Here's how to do it. Here's what research shows. Here's the evidence."

Guidance is relational: "Here's where I see you are. Here's what I notice happening. Here's what that might mean for your next move. Here's what I see when I look at you."

One can be delivered through a screen. You can watch a video at two in the morning and learn about the vagus nerve. You can read a book about somatic healing. You can download a PDF with ten strategies for nervous system regulation.

The other requires a kind of seeing—sustained, particular, warm—that is harder to scale. It requires someone paying attention to you. Not to your category or your problem type, but to you. To the specific way you pause when you talk about your mother. To the way your hands move when you describe what you actually want. To the particular weight of the piece you're trying to write.

A writer I know stopped listening to most writing podcasts because they all taught her more about what she already knew. What she needed was to sit with someone who understood the specific weight of the piece she was trying to write. Who could say, "This sentence is trying too hard. Let it be quieter." Not because there was a rule about sentence structure or style. But because she could feel in that moment that it was true. Because someone was looking at her work and seeing her work.

We're drowning in content and starving for orientation. The two are not in tension. They're not competing. Content without orientation is noise. A firehose. A room full of voices all talking at once. Orientation without content is vague encouragement, the kind that floats away before you can grasp it. The real work is in their combination—the particular seeing that comes from deep knowledge, applied to the specific person in front of you. The seeing that says: I know how this works. I've watched people move through this. I see where you are in that territory. Now let me help you understand what you're looking at.

The value of that is almost impossible to quantify.

And the economy keeps trying.

* * *

Here's what I think is happening to the meaning of value in this moment.

For most of the industrial era, value was tied to scarcity and effort. The harder something was to produce, the more it cost. The rarer the resource, the more it was worth. A handmade object held more value than a mass-produced one because someone had poured time and suffering into it. Calloused hands were evidence of worth. Exhaustion proved you mattered. An expert was valuable because their knowledge took years of grueling training to acquire. A book took months to write. Art took decades to master. The sweat was the product. The struggle was the credential. The equation was simple: effort equals worth. Suffering equals value.

This logic made sense. It aligned with how things actually worked. There were real constraints. Knowledge wasn't infinitely available. You couldn't learn surgery from a video. Handmade things required skill that took time to develop. A craftsperson's hands learned what the mind needed to know. Scarcity was real. Effort was necessary.

But the logic breaks down when the thing being produced is not scarce. When knowledge is infinite and instantly accessible. When ten thousand people can create the same thing at the same time. When the effort to create something becomes irrelevant to whether it actually helps anyone.

A book about productivity that took six months to write, with all the struggle and sleepless nights and tears, offers no more value than one that took two weeks and came easily if both confuse the reader in the same way. If both leave the reader feeling more lost than when they started. A course taught with suffering—the teacher burning themselves down in the service of comprehensive information—offers no more guidance than one taught with ease and warmth if both leave students feeling unmoored. A podcast series that required enormous effort and exhaustion to produce offers no more clarity than one that came easily if neither helps the listener understand where they actually are. The exhaustion of the maker doesn't transfer to the clarity of the receiver. Suffering is not an ingredient in guidance.

The old measure of value—how hard was it to make, how much did it cost to produce, how much suffering went into it—no longer tracks with reality. It's become a story we tell to justify pricing, to justify barriers to entry, to justify why some people get to matter more than others.

The new measure is becoming clear. It's not about the process. It's not about what it cost the maker. It's about the outcome. It's about what lands.

Does this help me feel less lost?

That's it. That's the question everything comes down to.

Does this help me know where I am? Does this help me understand what I'm feeling? Does this help me see the path that was obscured before? Does this make me feel less alone in what I'm experiencing? Does this orient me? Does this move me from confusion to clarity, even one degree?

If yes, it's valuable. If no, it isn't. It doesn't matter how much effort went into it. It doesn't matter how many hours the creator sacrificed. It doesn't matter if they suffered.

Not valuable as a status symbol or a credential or proof of effort or evidence that you suffered enough to deserve attention or have the right to charge money.

Valuable as orientation. As clarity. As the moment when the fever breaks and you can think again. When the fog lifts and you recognize the terrain. When you realize you're not crazy. When someone names it and you know it's true.

The work of creating that orientation is often subtle. It can look easy. A sentence that takes five minutes to write but lands because of everything that came before it. Because of every book the writer read, every conversation they listened to, every time they paid attention to what was actually happening. A question that seems simple but opens a door that's been stuck for years. A way of seeing that feels obvious once it's been named but was invisible before. A reflection that mirrors back to someone exactly what they've been unable to see. The invisible made visible. The unsayable made sayable.

This is the skill that matters now. Not the ability to produce through suffering. Not the ability to burn yourself up in the service of a project. Not the ability to collapse yourself in the name of doing good work. The skill that matters now is the ability to see clearly and speak that seeing in a way that helps someone else see. Clarity shared is clarity doubled. Seeing witnessed becomes seeing confirmed.

And here's what's strange, what breaks the logic of the old economy: This skill gets lighter as you develop it, not heavier. The more you practice seeing, the less energy it takes. The more clearly you see, the less effort the expression requires. Like a musician whose fingers finally know the piece so well that virtuosity looks like ease.

* * *

I had a conversation with a painter who'd been working in her practice for twenty years. She was struggling with a new piece, something that wasn't resolving, and she sat with a younger artist and explained what she was seeing in the canvas that wasn't yet visible. She talked about the color underneath the color. About the gesture that was trying to emerge. About what the painting was asking for instead of what the rules said it should do.

The younger artist listened and then asked: "How did you learn to see like that?"

The painter paused. She set down her coffee. Then she said: "Not by suffering more. By paying attention more. And by being willing to fail in front of people I trusted."

She'd spent decades learning to see. And the artifact of that seeing—the ability to point out what was actually happening in a canvas instead of what should be happening according to the rules—that skill was portable. She could teach it. She could apply it. She could offer it without it costing her anything but attention.

In fact, the more she used it, the sharper it became. The more she helped someone see, the more precisely she could see herself.

This is the opposite of the effort economy. In the effort economy, the more you give, the more depleted you become. You have a finite amount of capacity, and when you spend it, it's gone. This creates the logic of sacrifice: If I suffer enough, if I deplete myself enough, then I've earned something. Then I'm valuable. Then I have the right to exist in a way that matters.

But orientation works differently. The more you see clearly, the more you can see clearly. The more you name what's true, the truer your voice becomes. The more you help someone feel less lost, the less lost you are. It doesn't deplete you. It clarifies you. It strengthens the very capacity you're using.

It's not a zero-sum economy. It's an economy of accumulation. Of return. Of the strange gift that comes when you stop treating your seeing as a commodity and start treating it as a way of being alive.

Your value was never in your suffering. It was in your seeing. And seeing gets clearer, not dimmer, when you stop treating it as a form of punishment and start treating it as a form of love.

* * *

A therapist I know told me about a session with a long-term client. The client had finally, after years, decided to stop overworking. To set a boundary with her business. To claim back some of her time. It was the thing she said she wanted, and it terrified her completely.

The client came in looking shaken. Her hands were trembling slightly. She said, "I set the boundary. And the panic I feel is... it's not about the work. It's about who I am if I'm not doing it."

The therapist didn't offer reassurance. Didn't say, "You're more than your work." That's true and it's useless when you're in the pit of existential panic. It bounces off. It doesn't land.

Instead, she said: "The person you are when you're not working isn't a mystery. You already know who that is. You've just been too busy to notice."

And the client felt the shift. Not as philosophy. As reality. As recognition.

Because the therapist had been paying attention. Had been noticing, across sessions, the small moments when the client relaxed slightly. When her humor emerged—dry and quick and true. When she said something honest about what she actually wanted instead of what she thought she should do. When she made a joke about her family that revealed she was still in there, the person underneath the productivity.

The therapist was holding that version of the client—the one that was visible in glimpses—and saying, I see her. She's here. I've been watching her. She shows up when you stop trying so hard.

That's not insight. That's not a therapeutic technique or a clever reframe. That's orientation. It's someone saying: You're already whole. You just can't see it right now. Let me stand here where I can see and tell you what I'm looking at.

* * *

Let's be precise about what this means, because the current culture loves to take something clear and make it fuzzy. Loves to make things easier than they actually are.

When I say value is measured by orientation, not effort, I'm not saying that the work doesn't matter. I'm not saying that you can phone it in and still help someone. I'm not saying that the ability to see clearly emerges without the hard work of seeing. That insight comes without labor.

What I'm saying is that the hard work of seeing is not punishment. It's not something you suffer through in order to be worthy. It's not a payment you make to earn the right to matter. It's the actual work. The labor of attention. The discipline of looking at something until you understand it not as an intellectual exercise but as a lived thing. The commitment to being present with what is actually happening.

That work is real. It's difficult. It's just not dramatic. It doesn't look like struggle. It looks like someone paying attention. Watching. Listening. Asking better questions. Noticing small things. Showing up again and again, even when there's no external reward for doing so.

And when you do that work, the value that emerges is real and transportable and useful.

A writer who has read widely and thought carefully about her subject can write a useful essay in a day. A therapist who has done their own work and paid attention to thousands of hours of human struggle can help someone find their way in a single session. A teacher who knows their field completely can deliver clarity that lands because it comes from understanding, not from following a script. A friend who has learned to pay attention can say the one thing that changes everything.

The effort happens. It's just not visible. And that's okay. The visibility was never the point.

The point is whether someone on the other end feels less lost. Whether they can stand on the ground they're actually standing on. Whether they can hear themselves thinking again.

* * *

This is where the book turns.

Because Part I was about understanding how you got here. How the effort economy took root in you. How your nervous system learned to be suspicious of ease and comfort and rest. How the fusion of your worth with your productivity happened, and why it made sense at the time. Why it kept you alive.

That's all true. And it's all behind you now.

From here, we're going to talk about what you actually are when you're not exhausted. What becomes visible when you stop performing. What your nervous system knows that your mind hasn't caught up to yet. What you want when you're not scared. What you see when you're not running.

We're going to talk about the kind of value that doesn't require your suffering. The kind of value that emerges from clarity and stays even when the effort stops. The kind of value that gets stronger when you're rested, not weaker. That becomes more precise when you're calm.

But first, you have to let yourself be here. To feel what's happening in this moment. To notice what it's like to be seen and named instead of fixed and improved. To experience the difference between being told you're okay and feeling yourself become okay because someone is looking at you and not flinching.

Some people describe this moment as relief. Some describe it as disorientation. Some people feel it as a strange lightness in the chest, like something heavy has finally been put down. Some people feel the opposite—a sinking, a settling, a weight that was being held by adrenaline finally making contact with the ground.

What do you feel? Where in your body does it live? What happens if you sit with it instead of moving away from it? What if this feeling, exactly as it is, is not a problem to be solved but a threshold you're standing on?

That's the question we're asking now.

Chapter Six

The Myth of Visible Labor

The surgeon finishes at 9:47 a.m. Forty-one minutes. The patient is closed, stable, already headed to recovery. Her hands are steady as she documents the procedure. No tremor. No performance of exhaustion. She sets the pen down with the same deliberate care she used at the beginning of the surgery, which suggests nothing, which suggests everything.

In the surgeon's lounge, a colleague asks how it went. "Clean," she says. "Everything cooperated." She's standing at the window overlooking the parking lot, her scrubs still damp at the collar. She sips water. Her voice is level, conversational, the voice of someone talking about lunch rather than the small miracle of anatomy she just orchestrated.

What the colleague sees: efficiency. What the colleague suspects: luck. What the colleague absolutely will not believe: that forty-one minutes of work at this caliber required decades of calibration that lives now in muscle memory and pattern recognition so refined it feels like instinct. That the work was *more* difficult to earn, not less difficult to perform. That the hands moving through space at that speed were doing more complex problem-solving than his hands moving slowly through the same motions, conscious of each step, still checking, still verifying, still laboring.

He has been working for eighteen years. She has been working for thirty-two. The time difference contains the whole truth of the myth.

The myth of visible labor says that real work has a shape you can see. Sweat. Hours. Struggle rendered visible. The person at the desk until midnight is working. The person who leaves at five has somehow cheated. The hands that show calluses contain evidence of commitment. The hands that don't—those hands are suspect. We have been trained to believe that cost equals value, that the difficulty of a thing measures its worth, that the person who suffers most has earned most.

This bias is not accidental. We inherited it from economies built on physical visibility. If you haul stone, the wall proves your labor. If you swing a hammer, the nails driven are countable. If you work a loom, the cloth accumulates hour by hour. Industrial capitalism trained us to trust the observable: the time clock, the assembly line, the output measured in units per hour, the visible proof of motion that equals productivity. Visibility became the currency of credibility. A person who moved was a person who was accomplishing something. A person who stood still, or who sat quietly, or whose labor happened in the interior of the mind—that person required explanation.

Then skill entered the equation, and the myth cracked but did not break.

* * *

A pianist practices eight hours daily. The hands move across keys in patterns that look nearly automatic, as if the body is playing itself, as if she is merely an audience to her own movements. Each repetition is not redundant; it is architecture. The neural pathway deepens. The synaptic connections thicken. The cognitive load for that specific passage drops from conscious problem-solving to embodied knowledge. The piece that once required her full attention now requires only monitoring, the way you monitor your own breathing—you know it is happening, you can adjust it if needed, but you do not have to think about each separate inhale and exhale.

To an observer, it looks like she's playing the same piece over again. What's actually happening is compression. The work is not disappearing. It is condensing into competence. The deciding happens faster. The mistakes get caught earlier. The thinking shrinks down and relocates from the prefrontal cortex to the cerebellum, from the front of the brain where conscious reasoning lives to the back, where automatic expertise lives. By hour six, her mind is wandering. She is thinking about dinner. She is humming something else entirely. And the piece is still being executed at a level of accuracy and nuance that would require a beginner's full attention to even comprehend.

This is the mechanism that makes visible labor become invisible labor.

Mastery is integration. The thinking still happens—pattern recognition, micro-adjustment, real-time problem-solving, constant tiny corrections happening at speeds too fast for consciousness to track—but it happens at a speed and fluidity that reads as effortlessness to anyone watching. The surgeon's forty-one minutes contain more decision-making than a resident's four hours. The decisions happen faster. They are stacked tighter. They live in the body as much as the mind, which means they live in the nervous system, in the hands' memory, in the eye's ability to recognize deviation before the mind has consciously named it.

Competence looks deceptively simple because it is no longer labored. That is what makes it competence. Incompetence is visible. Competence is transparent.

But here is what we do with this: we discount it. The pianist thinks, "That went smoothly." She translates smoothly into easy, then easy into not-real. "I barely had to think." The words come before the analysis. She has absorbed the cultural story that visible struggle is the only legitimate struggle, which means that when the struggle becomes internal, invisible, integrated—when it moves into her body and stops being audible to external judgment—she mistakes this for an absence of difficulty rather than a transformation of it. She mistakes the silence of effort for the silence of laziness.

The work compressed does not feel like work anymore. It feels like facility. Like she's just naturally talented. Like it wasn't really effort at all. Like the eight hours are just her spending time at the piano because she loves it, not because she is still doing something that looks easy only because she has spent eight thousand hours—ten thousand, twenty thousand—learning how to make it look easy.

* * *

This is where the myth eats its own logic.

If visible labor is the measure of legitimacy, then the people who have done the most work become the people who can least prove it. The surgeon's forty-one minutes is evidence against her—it looks too easy. The athlete whose movements appear fluid and inevitable has trained in ways that are now invisible. The writer who produces clean prose on the first pass has integrated years of revision into her thought process before the first word hits the page. She is not writing less than the person who produces five drafts. She is writing faster because the editing now occurs simultaneously with the composition. The revising happens during the thinking happens during the writing happens all at once, so fast that it looks like there is no revising at all.

The person producing it knows this is not laziness. Knows the work is still there. But the world has trained her to doubt her own knowledge when there is no visible evidence to support it. So she performs evidence. She stays up late even when she could finish earlier, because late nights prove commitment. She shows her struggle in early drafts even when she could wait to share the refined version, because rough work looks more honest than smooth work. She becomes less efficient in order to appear more legitimate. She manufactures visibility because invisibility reads as absence.

In a coffee shop, a copywriter overhears a client on the phone. "I can turn these ads around by tomorrow morning," she says. A pause. "No, I'm not rushing it. That's just how long it takes." Another pause, longer. The copywriter knows the client is skeptical. The client is thinking: if it's that fast, is it any good? The copywriter could say: I've been writing copy for fourteen years. I could say: I've internalized every principle of persuasion, every pattern of response, every psychological lever that makes words work. I could perform my difficulty. Instead, she says nothing. She hangs up. She delivers tomorrow.

The work is complete. It exists. The fact that it now appears simple is not its failure. But this is not comfortable for anyone involved. The person producing it becomes vulnerable to her own doubt. The people observing it become vulnerable to misjudging it. We live in a culture that does not have a category for "legitimate labor that looks easy." So we invented suspicion as a substitute. So we built systems that require struggle as a component of proof.

* * *

I want to separate this from the common narrative about "showing your work" or "being vulnerable." That is not what is happening here. The surgeon does not need to perform her competence by describing her struggles. She does not need a confessional about how she got here. She needs to trust that forty-one minutes of intelligent action has value regardless of its duration. The pianist does not need to explain her practice hours to justify her performance. The copywriter does not need to narrate her process. The work is complete. The fact that it appears simple is not its failure. It is its success.

But this creates a particular kind of loneliness. The person producing the work cannot share the realness of what she's doing because the realness is invisible. The work that would most benefit from acknowledgment is the work that least appears to need it. So she keeps working. She keeps delivering. She watches people misunderstand her capacity as a kind of accident, some combination of natural gift and favorable circumstances, rather than as the result of ten thousand hours of compression.

* * *

Enter artificial intelligence, which compresses visible labor in a way that disrupts everyone simultaneously.

The person who writes with an AI tool and produces a clean document in two hours faces the same accusation the surgeon faces, the pianist faces, the experienced writer faces: that the ease indicates illegitimacy. That the work was somehow not real work because it did not look like work. That the thinking did not happen because the thinking was not visible. That something has been stolen or cut or shortened. That shortcuts have been taken.

There is something interesting happening here, something that reveals the entire architecture of the myth. The person with decades of writing experience who produces fast, clean work is trusted (eventually) because we know the decades are there, even if we don't see them. The person using AI to produce fast, clean work is not trusted because we know the decades are not there—but the thinking still happened. It just happened elsewhere. The compression was borrowed from a different source. The labor was done, but not by the person holding the pen.

The accusation is identical. The compression is identical. The source of the compression is different.

But the identity disruption is also identical, and this is where the myth reveals its real architecture. We have not been measuring work at all. We have been measuring suffering. And when suffering becomes optional, we don't have a language for what remains. When the person can get to the end without the visible pain, we cannot calibrate whether they have actually arrived.

A person writes with AI and thinks: this was too easy, so it is not really work. A person writes without AI and thinks: this was hard, so it is really work. The measure, in both cases, is the person's own discomfort. The work itself—the thinking, the selection, the judgment, the revision—is secondary to the sensation of having had to struggle through it. The work's reality becomes contingent on the worker's suffering. Remove the suffering, and the work becomes suspect, even to the worker herself.

The myth of visible labor is actually the myth of visible suffering. And we have organized entire identity structures around it. We have built careers on the assumption that difficulty is the proof. That the harder the work is to do, the more legitimate it is. That suffering is not a bug in the system—it is a feature. It is the evidence. It is the seal of legitimacy.

* * *

Let me be direct: if you are still struggling with your core work in your forties the way you struggled with it in your twenties, something is wrong. Not with you. With your trajectory.

Expertise should feel lighter over time. The thinking should get faster. The decisions should become more automatic. The process should compress. This is not laziness. This is the spine of your development. If you are working harder every year instead of differently every year, you have either stopped learning or stopped doing the thing you actually know how to do. You have either plateaued or you have lost faith in your own competence.

The discomfort of this statement is worth sitting with for a moment. Let it sit. We have made achievement narratives almost entirely about difficulty. The person who overcomes the most is the person who suffered the most. The person whose work looks effortless is suspect. We have built cultures and careers around proving our worth through visible strain. We have made suffering the metric. We have made pain the price of legitimacy.

But a surgeon who still takes four hours to do a procedure she should be able to do in forty-one minutes is not demonstrating commitment. She is demonstrating something closer to the opposite. She has not yet converted her knowledge into skill. She is still conscious of every step. Her competence has not compressed. She is still laboring where she should be fluent. This is not dedication. It is stagnation. It is the refusal to move past visible labor into the territory where the real work happens.

This is true for writers and designers and therapists and teachers and engineers. For anyone whose work compounds over time, whose competence deepens through repetition. The compression is not the failure point. The compression is the entire point. The person who learns to work faster, smarter, with less visible effort—that person is the person who has actually learned. The person who still struggles with the same problems they struggled with five years ago has not actually learned them. They have just learned how to perform learning.

* * *

Now we have to talk about internalization. Because the myth of visible labor is not just something other people believe about you. It is something you believe about yourself. It becomes a story you tell yourself, a narrative that your own mind has accepted as true.

The experienced person stops attributing her speed to competence. She attributes it to luck, to the particular conditions of this project, to the fact that this one came together—implying that the others, the harder ones, the ones that required more visible effort, those were somehow more legitimately work. She has absorbed the cultural story so completely that her own fluency reads as an exception rather than a pattern. The easy wins become anomalies. The difficult wins become the baseline truth.

Then the younger person watches this and thinks: she doesn't work hard. She's just naturally talented. What the younger person cannot see—what *cannot* be seen—is the decades of compression that made natural talent appear. The work was done. It is being done. It just looks different now. It looks like the work is not happening at all. It looks like she is moving through the world in some effortless way that the younger person has not yet achieved and probably never will.

Mastery is invisible because mastery is integration. The thinking gets woven into the doing so tightly that you cannot separate them for observation. The person cannot explain how she does the thing because the how has become automatic, has moved below the level of language. This is not a problem to solve. This is the condition of being skilled. This is what competence actually looks like when you strip away the performance.

In a music studio, a producer watches a session musician record a part on the third take. The musician shrugs and packs up. The producer asks: don't you want to do more? "I got it," the musician says. The producer is not satisfied. He wants to see labor. He wants to see struggle. He wants to see the musician working until the part is perfect. What he does not understand is that perfection, for this musician, takes three takes. That this is what thirty years of playing sounds like. That the work happened over three decades, not across three hours. That the compression is complete.

* * *

There is a parallel between the person who becomes a master craftsperson and the person who learns to work with AI tools effectively. Both are compressing visible labor. Both are replacing the repetitive parts of the work with something faster, smoother, more automated. The craftsperson's automation lives in their nervous system. The person with AI tools is borrowing someone else's automation. But the compression is structurally the same. Both generate the same suspicion. Both trigger the same accusation: this is too easy to be legitimate.

The accusations are not equivalent. One person has earned the right to efficiency through years of practice. The other is using a tool that offers efficiency as a shortcut. But the identity disruption is identical. Both are no longer struggling with the thing they are producing. Both are freed from the visible labor. Both have to grieve what that means—the loss of proof, the loss of visible evidence, the loss of the suffering that used to demonstrate their worth.

And both have to decide whether to trust their own knowledge that the work is still happening, or whether to perform struggle in order to appease the myth. Both have to ask themselves: what am I willing to sacrifice on the altar of appearing legitimate?

* * *

Here is what the myth costs us: it keeps us tethered to difficulty as a proxy for value.

The person who has finally learned her craft and begun to move through it with ease does not get to simply enjoy this. She has to defend it. She has to prove that her speed is not a sign that she is cutting corners, that the ease is not a sign that she is being less careful, that the absence of visible suffering is not a sign that she is avoiding real responsibility. The world requires her to perform her difficulty in order to trust her work.

So she stays up late even though she could finish earlier. She shows the rough drafts. She narrates the problems. She makes visible what would otherwise compress. She does not do this because she suddenly became incapable of finishing earlier. She does this because she has absorbed the requirement to appear to be struggling in order to appear to be legitimate. She has internalized the demand for proof. She has built her own cage and locked herself inside it.

This is the real cost of the myth: not just the doubt, but the performance required to manage the doubt. The reduction of efficiency in order to appear efficient. The addition of suffering to prove you are not lazy. The visible labor you have to add on top of the work you have already done, just to make the work readable as real work. The competence you have to disguise in order to be believed.

* * *

The liberation, then, is in a simple reorientation: cost is not the same as value.

A procedure that takes forty-one minutes is not worth less than a procedure that takes four hours. The thinking did not happen less. It happened faster. It happened more fluidly. It was more integrated. This is what makes it worth more, not less. The speed is the evidence of mastery, not the evidence of cutting corners. Compression is the achievement, not the shortcut.

The same reorientation applies to writing, to design, to any skilled work that compounds over time. If you have been practicing a thing for ten years, and it now takes you two weeks to do what once took you six months, you are not working less hard. You are working more intelligently. Your labor has not disappeared. It has been absorbed into competence. Competence looks simple because simplicity is its entire point. The work has become so integrated that it appears automatic. This appearance is not deception. It is accuracy.

And if someone suspects you based on the ease of your work, that is their problem to solve, not yours. You do not have to perform suffering to prove your legitimacy. You do not have to add struggle to your process in order to make your skill readable. Your competence is not enhanced by visible labor. It is compromised by it. Every moment you spend manufacturing struggle is a moment you are not spending on the work itself.

The myth of visible labor keeps people from becoming excellent because excellence, by definition, is invisible. The person who is still struggling with the fundamentals is still visible. The person who has integrated the fundamentals is not. This is why we respect the struggle and discount the ease. We can see the struggle. We cannot see what comes after it. But what comes after it is everything. That is where the actual work happens.

* * *

Skill becoming craft becoming expression. This is the trajectory. The early stage is all visible labor. The person consciously moving through each step. The thinking is loud. The mistakes are visible. The struggle is transparent. This looks like working hard because it is working hard. The effort and the labor are not yet separated. The person is not yet skilled enough to hide the work from view.

Then something shifts. The work does not get easier in the sense of becoming less demanding. It gets easier in the sense of becoming more automatic. The conscious steps compress. The thinking gets faster. The mistakes become smaller, rarer, more easily corrected in real-time without the person having to stop and recalibrate. The labor is still there. It is just no longer visible. This stage is unstable. The person is no longer sure they are working hard enough because they cannot see their own effort. The doubt creeps in. The world reinforces this doubt. They begin to perform struggle in order to feel legitimate. They add the rough drafts. They narrate the difficulties. They stay up late. They manufacture evidence.

Then, if they stay with it, another shift. The work becomes expression. The integration is so complete that the person is no longer aware of the process at all. They are aware only of the thing itself, the work emerging. The labor has not disappeared. It has become so compressed, so woven into the action itself, that there is no longer a distinction between thinking and doing, between process and product. This is where the work becomes sustainable, becomes generative, becomes the thing they actually do with their life rather than the thing they have to do in order to prove something. The work becomes alive.

This trajectory is not comfortable. It requires releasing the proof of your own legitimacy. It requires trusting your own knowledge when the world has no framework for understanding invisible work. It requires not performing the struggle that made you appear legitimate in the earlier stages. It requires believing that your competence is enough without visible evidence that you earned it. It requires a kind of faith.

Most people do not make it here because the passage from visible labor to invisible mastery requires passing through a stage where nobody believes you are working at all. The doubt is not external. It is internal. The person producing the work looks at her own ease and thinks: this is not real. This cannot be real. I should be struggling more. I should be visible. I should be able to prove this is happening.

So she manufactures visibility. She adds the rough drafts. She narrates the thinking. She performs the difficulty. She remains caught in visible labor not because she cannot move past it, but because she cannot trust that moving past it is safe. Not because she lacks the skill, but because she lacks the belief that invisible skill counts.

* * *

But here is what I know: the work that has integrated into your body, into your nervous system, into your automatic knowing—that work is the realest work you will ever do. That is the work that matters. That is the work that changes things. That is the work you were actually meant to do.

Everything before that is getting ready. Everything after that is just life.

The myth of visible labor wants you to stay in the getting-ready stage. It wants the struggle to remain transparent. It wants to be able to see your effort, to count your hours, to measure your pain. Because the moment your work compresses, the moment it becomes invisible, nobody can verify that you are still working at all. Nobody can count the value. Nobody can measure the worth. You have to do that for yourself. You have to believe it without external proof. You have to stand in the knowing.

This is terrifying. This is also liberation.

Release the performance. The competence is enough. The work is real regardless of whether anyone can see it happening. The fact that it looks easy now is not proof that it is easy. It is proof that you have finally become excellent at it. It is proof that you have done the real work, the invisible work, the work that matters.

And excellence, by definition, looks like grace.

Chapter Seven

From Effort-Based Identity to Competence-Based Identity

The body knows first. A woman at forty-three notices her shoulders have dropped. Not as metaphor—they've physically migrated downward in her frame. For twenty years they lived near her ears, tensed against the next crisis, the next missed deadline, the next moment when someone would need her to solve something that shouldn't have broken in the first place. Her shoulders kept her small and reactive, a coiled thing ready to deploy. Now they rest. They hang differently. She catches her reflection in the bathroom mirror and the shape is unfamiliar, like looking at someone she used to know. The person in the mirror is wider somehow, not in weight but in presence. There's a slack in the muscles where there used to be strings.

This is what it looks like when the effort identity begins to dissolve.

Not all at once. Not with fanfare. The crack appears quietly, often in midlife when everything else is already shifting—children old enough now to solve their own problems, bodies betraying bargains made in youth, relationships recalibrating under the weight of their own duration. A person gets good at their work. Really good. Good enough that the problems begin to solve themselves before they crystallize into crises. The late nights are no longer required. The heroic recoveries feel repetitive, like playing the same piece on the same instrument until it becomes muscle memory rather than music. One morning you realize you've answered the same question three different ways for three different people, and on the fourth iteration, something flickers. A small, dangerous thing: boredom.

Bored. In the work you built your entire identity around.

The effort-based identity is built on friction. It feeds on resistance—problems to overcome, obstacles to work around or punch through, a constant condition of being needed in that particular way that requires you to live in crisis mode. The identity says: I am valuable because I suffer for what matters. I am reliable because I show up when the stakes are unbearable. I am worthy because I have sacrificed things that other people would have kept. The whole structure is a machine that runs on scarcity and urgency. It's why the effort identity can feel so clean, so morally certain. It has rules. Do the thing even when you don't want to. Push when you're tired. Ask for help last. Never admit something is easy. The identity knows how to win in a scarcity mindset because the scarcity mindset is the air it breathes.

Then you get good. And the air changes.

A man who built a career on fixing broken systems reaches a threshold where he's fixed enough of them that he understands the architecture beneath the breakdown. He sees the problems before they metastasize. He has people who trust his judgment without needing proof. The work is still consequential—maybe more so—but it no longer feels dangerous. The danger is gone and the danger was the entire point. When I ask him what his days look like now, he says, "Mostly I show up and the thing gets done well. And then—" He makes a gesture that looks like releasing something into water. "Nothing. Silence." He's not happy about this. He's not unhappy either. He's troubled. The nothing troubles him more than the chaos ever did.

This is the gap where grief lives.

The competence-based identity is emerging—calmer, more discerning, less prone to the adrenaline spikes that the old identity mistook for aliveness. But the competence identity doesn't have drama. It doesn't have the built-in validation system that crisis provides. A job done well, completed cleanly, without fanfare or last-minute heroics—it disappears into the background like a well-hung door that closes without noise. People don't gather around competence. They do gather around crisis. Competence is a solo thing. It's you and the work and the internal knowledge that it's done right. That's supposed to be enough.

For people who used the effort identity's drama as a regulating mechanism, it isn't.

* * *

The effort-based identity was a container. Whatever was happening in the person underneath—the restlessness, the shame, the deep conviction that they were inadequate—could be held inside the container of being busy and needed. The container said: you're not failing, you're fighting. You're not lost, you're solving problems. You're not empty, you're depleted. Every problem became a place to pour the nervous energy that had nowhere else to go. The crises weren't just external events requiring solutions. They were internal rescues disguised as external ones. The person was using the work as a way to escape the smaller voice that whispered you're not enough.

When the external crises no longer come, the internal ones don't have their outlet.

A woman in her late forties realizes that her body is reaching for stress that no longer exists. There's a place in her chest that's looking for something specific—the cortisol hit, the spike of adrenaline that meant I am doing something important right now. She exercises, trying to exhaust herself into sleep. She finds herself creating small dramas, magnifying minor conflicts with colleagues, finding reasons to worry about things she's already handled. She refreshes her email at midnight looking for problems that need solving. She's grieving, but she doesn't know that's what this is. She thinks she's failing. She thinks she's failing at the transition to being less busy, which is its own bitter irony. She's still trying to achieve ease the way she achieved exhaustion—through force, through will, through the sheer determination that used to solve everything. Her body wants the familiar burn of cortisol the way an athlete's body wants the familiar pain of exertion. It knows that feeling. It knows how to respond to that feeling. The silence is a foreign language.

The shift from effort-based to competence-based is not a promotion.

It's a fundamental reorganization of the nervous system. The old system ran hot. Cortisol and adrenaline and the particular clarity that comes when the stakes feel high. The body in this state is responsive, reactive, ready. It can work for long periods because the stress hormones are keeping it upright, keeping the focus sharp. The person can justify staying in this state indefinitely because there's always another crisis, always another person who needs the thing only they can provide. The martyrdom is exquisite. The martyrdom is also the entire identity.

The new system—the competence system—runs differently. It's not lazy or passive. It's discerning. It looks at a problem and says: this is not mine to solve. It examines a request and says: this doesn't align with what I'm meant to do now. It encounters a situation and recognizes: someone else's kind of attention is needed here, not mine. It creates distance between stimulus and response. It makes room for the knowledge that doing something well is not the same as doing everything. The competence system is not running away from difficulty—it's choosing which difficulties are still instructive, which ones actually deserve the finite amount of attention a person has to give.

But the body doesn't trust what it can't feel accelerating.

* * *

There's a grief in this that culture gives almost no language for. We have language for failing at our work, for burning out, for finally saying enough. We celebrate the sabbatical, the career pivot, the person who chooses family over ambition. But we don't have language for the person who got so good at their work that the work stopped requiring them to be heroic, and they discovered that heroism was the only narrative they knew. We don't honor what is being released when someone outgrows the identity that has kept them safe.

Because it did keep them safe. The effort-based identity was not a lie. It was a solution. It worked, and like all solutions that work for a long time, it worked until it stopped working. Then it became a cage.

This is not a metaphor. It's somatic. The person can feel the cage. They can feel it around their ribs like a corset that's been tightened for so long the person forgot it was there until someone undid the laces slightly and suddenly the weight of it became visible. They can feel their hands looking for a problem to grab the way a smoker's hands look for a cigarette. They can feel the absence of the narrative that made them coherent. Who am I if I am not struggling. Who am I if I am not useful. Who am I if I don't have proof of my worth embedded in my exhaustion. These aren't rhetorical questions. They're the shape of panic.

The Jungian language for this is individuation. The persona—the mask, the role, the "I am the reliable one"—is dissolving not through failure but through integration. The shadow—the part that knows how to rest, to create without an audience, to be moved by things that have no practical outcome—is pressing at the borders of consciousness. The shadow is not the enemy. In Jungian work, the shadow is everything the conscious identity has had to disown to maintain its shape. For the effort-based person, the shadow contains the capacity for ease, for stillness, for desires that don't have a purpose beyond themselves. The shadow is interested in things because they're beautiful. The shadow takes a walk and doesn't need it to be exercise. The shadow knows how to receive without earning.

The conscious identity finds this terrifying.

Integrating the shadow doesn't mean becoming it. It means allowing it to move from the unconscious edges into the available spectrum of self. It means the person becomes larger, more complicated, less dependent on a single narrative to prove their worth. But the process isn't comfortable. The persona doesn't dissolve gently. It dissolves in waves of grief because it is grief—releasing a version of self that was entirely loyal, that protected the person, that meant something clear in a complicated world. The grief is for the loss of certainty as much as anything else. The effort-based identity knew exactly what was required. Get up, push, sacrifice, prove. The competence-based identity is messier. It requires judgment. It requires knowing the difference between rest and avoidance, between discernment and laziness, between saying no to something and abandoning responsibility. The old identity never asked these questions. The new one asks them all the time.

* * *

This transition often lands in the middle years—when bodies are already changing, when the children who required parental heroics are moving toward independence, when marriages either deepen into genuine knowledge or fracture under the accumulated weight of performance. The work identity crisis doesn't happen in a vacuum. It happens in a season when the entire sense of necessary usefulness is under renegotiation. The person is losing the role of indispensable at work just as they're losing the role of essential to their teenagers. The body is losing its reliability just as the external systems that required their particular kind of managing are solving themselves. Every tier of the structure is shifting simultaneously.

Some people experience this as a collapse. The identity structure cracks and they fall through it, lost and unmoored, with no idea how to rebuild. They swing hard the other way—quitting the job, abandoning the work identity entirely, trying to force themselves into something that looks like ease but feels like freefall. They're still trying to achieve it through force. They're still at war.

Others move through it with the kind of attention that looks like what it actually is: a funeral for a self that served well.

A man I know spent his forties in what I can only describe as a particular kind of honoring. He didn't quit his work, but he changed his relationship to it. He let himself feel what he was losing—the clarity of being needed in that specific way, the nobility of the sacrifice, the strange morality of exhaustion that had made him feel like a good person. He talked about the person he had been with the kind of love you feel for something you're releasing. Not sentimentality. Real love. The kind of love you feel when you watch someone you've known your whole life walk away because it's time for both of you. He didn't perform the transformation. He lived it, slowly, in real time, with his shoulders eventually dropping and his insomnia eventually easing and his need to create small crises gradually, actually, genuinely loosening.

What happened on the other side of that was something the effort-based identity couldn't have imagined: clarity that didn't come with adrenaline. The work got better. The person got clearer about what actually needed his attention and what he'd been carrying out of obligation or because he didn't know how to put it down. The competence identity doesn't require the same amount of suffering to prove its point. It just does the thing well and doesn't need a standing ovation for it.

But getting here requires moving through the grief.

The body has to grieve what it's losing—the hormone hits, the clarity of being in crisis, the specific kind of visibility that comes from being the one who solves the unsolvable. The identity has to grieve the narrative that held it together. The psyche has to grieve the persona because even though the persona was built on a partial truth, it was a truth. The effort-based person was reliable. They did show up. They did sacrifice. Releasing that identity means acknowledging that those things were real and that they no longer define what is necessary.

There's a particular kind of tenderness that's required here. Not the saccharine kind. Not the kind that says "you're doing amazing, bestie." The tenderness that comes from honoring what something was before it becomes something else. The tenderness of a real goodbye. The kind you feel when someone you love is leaving and you're genuinely glad they're going because they need to, but you feel the loss of them anyway.

* * *

Many people skip this part. They try to rewrite the story retroactively—deciding the effort-based identity was toxic all along, that they were always going to outgrow it, that the new competence identity is obviously superior. This is its own form of violence. It erases what the effort-based identity actually did, which was keep the person functioning when they didn't know how to function any other way. The effort-based identity didn't fail. It succeeded. It got the person here.

And now here requires something different.

The competence-based identity includes what came before. It doesn't pretend the struggle was useless or that suffering was enlightenment. But it does say: the struggle got you somewhere. You learned something in that furnace. You developed capacities that were real. And you've outgrown the furnace. You don't need it anymore. The grief is in releasing what you don't need anymore while honoring that it was necessary once.

A woman in her middle years describes the feeling like this: "I'm mourning someone who's still me." There's a particular condition in midlife—not crisis, but recalibration. The person is still here, still functional, still valuable. But the structure that made her feel valuable has fundamentally reorganized. She has to relearn what evidence of her worth looks like when it's not measured in sacrifice. She has to relearn how to feel like herself when the self she feels like is doing less and accomplishing more.

This is why the transition from effort-based to competence-based is not just an identity shift. It's a spiritual one. Not in the religious sense, but in the sense of individuation—the deepening integration of a human being becoming more wholly themselves. The effort-based identity was a necessary exile. It was self-protection. It was brilliance applied to survival. The competence-based identity is what's possible on the other side of survival. It's freedom disguised as boredom until the person learns to recognize freedom when it doesn't come with adrenaline.

The shoulders drop. The email refresh becomes less frequent. There are moments—long moments, eventually—when the silence is not an absence. It's a fullness. Not because the work is less important, but because the person has finally done enough of it that they can stop proving something. They can just do it because it's what they do. They can walk into their office and know that the competence is there, that the knowledge is there, that they don't need to prove it again.

This is not the end of struggle. It's the end of struggle as proof.

* * *

It's the end of needing the world to recognize your sacrifice in order to believe in yourself. It's the end of running hot. It's the end of using crisis as proof of aliveness. The work continues. The struggle continues in different forms—the struggle to say no, the struggle to rest, the struggle to trust that you are enough without the exhaust fumes of urgency around you.

But the person is different now. Larger. Less certain, maybe, but more whole.

A man in his early fifties describes it this way, in a coffee shop near his office, his hands wrapped around a cup he doesn't rush to finish: "I used to know who I was. I was the guy who made it happen. That was clean. That was true. Now I'm—" He pauses. He's looking for the word. "I'm competent. I know things. But that's not a story. That's not a narrative people can follow. When I tell someone what I do now, they're less impressed because I make it look easy. And the thing is, I do make it look easy now. Because I've done it ten thousand times." He takes a sip. "I'm mourning the importance of the struggle more than I'm glad about the ease. That's the weird part. The ease is what I wanted, but I didn't know I was paying for it with relevance. With being needed."

The identity shift is not a moment. It's a series of small surrenders that accumulate until one day the person notices they're different. They notice it in how they respond to a crisis at work that would have consumed them five years ago. Now they assign it to someone else and sleep through the night. They notice it in how their body doesn't leap to attention when their phone buzzes. The nervous system has learned that the ping is not a directive. They notice it in meetings when they stay quiet because they genuinely have nothing to add, and the quiet doesn't feel like failure. It feels like discretion.

A woman I know keeps a journal from her thirties. She was in her mid-thirties then, running a nonprofit, sleeping four hours a night, the kind of person who would take on a whole project because she saw it wasn't getting done. She reads an entry from February: "I'm so tired but I can't stop. Who will take care of this if I don't." She's fifty-three now. She reads that sentence and it makes her cry, but not because she's ashamed of the woman who wrote it. She cries because she understands that woman now. That woman was doing the best thing she knew to do. She was using the only tool she had, which was her own relentless energy, her own refusal to let things fail. She was honorable. And she was also running on empty.

The woman at fifty-three doesn't run on empty anymore. She doesn't run on adrenaline. But sometimes she misses the electricity of it. She misses the person who would move mountains. That person was real. That person accomplished things. That person had a clarity of purpose that didn't require ambiguity or reflection.

The competence-based identity introduces ambiguity. It says: this is important, and it's not your responsibility to fix it. It says: you're capable, and no one needs you to be available at 2 a.m. It says: you've proven yourself, and you don't need to do it again.

The grief is in letting the old identity release its stranglehold on proof. The old identity had a measurement: did you exhaust yourself. Did you sacrifice. Did you put yourself last. If you did those things, you were valuable. The new identity's measurements are stranger. Did you do this well. Do you feel alignment. Are you working from something other than obligation. These measurements can't be tracked in the same way. There's no visible exhaustion to show for it. There's no drama to narrate.

* * *

Some people move through this transition so slowly it looks like it didn't happen at all. The shift is gradual enough that they don't have to consciously grieve it. They just one day realize they're someone different. The relief can come all at once, or it can come in fragments. The insomnia that haunted them for decades finally breaks. They take a vacation and don't think about work. They have a thought, and they don't immediately mobilize to solve whatever problem they imagined. The nervous system slowly learns that there isn't actually a tiger in the room.

Others hit a wall. The effort-based identity crashes, usually because the body finally refuses to cooperate. A heart problem. A complete breakdown. An injury that won't heal as quickly as it used to. The body vetoes the old arrangement. And then the person has no choice but to transition. They have no choice but to become someone else because the version they were is no longer viable.

And still others do both. They sense the change coming and they resist it until the body intervenes. They're conscious of the transition but unwilling, grieving but also furious, because part of them knows that the old identity is dying and they're not ready to let it go. They're not ready to become the kind of person who rests. They're not ready to be valued for competence instead of crisis. They're not ready to be invisible.

The invisibility is something no one talks about. When you're the person who solves crises, people see you. When you're the person who does things well, cleanly, without drama, you blend into the background. The work gets done. People benefit from it. But they don't know to thank you because they don't see the effort. It just appears to have happened naturally. And for the person who built an entire sense of identity around visibility, around being needed, around being seen to struggle, this invisibility can feel like erasure.

A woman who spent her career as a project manager describes what happened when she moved into a strategic role: "Nobody sees you anymore. You're not the one fixing things. You're the one suggesting that things be fixed differently, and whether that happens or not, no one knows you were the one who suggested it. I'm doing more important work now. I'm actually changing the system instead of just managing crises within it. But when I go home, I feel like I did nothing. I'm not exhausted. No one came to me with an emergency. Nothing blew up." She's describing the invisibility of competence. She's describing what it feels like to have impact without exhaustion, and how strange that is when exhaustion is what you learned to recognize as impact.

The transition requires that the person develops a new capacity for witnessing themselves. The effort-based identity is witnessed by others—they see the struggle, the sacrifice, the relentless energy. The competence-based identity has to be witnessed internally. The person has to know, without external confirmation, that they did well. That they made a difference. That they deserve rest because they deserve it, not because they've earned it through sacrifice.

* * *

This internal witness is not something most people have developed. The effort-based identity doesn't require it. It requires external validation. It requires being seen to struggle. When the external witness stops appearing—when people stop commenting on how hard you work, when the crisis management stops, when you transition into a role where your value is assumed rather than visible—the person has to learn to witness themselves. And that's work. That's real work, maybe harder than the original crisis management because it requires a kind of attention that culture doesn't teach us.

A man who made this transition in his mid-forties describes it: "I had to learn to be proud of things no one would ever know about. A decision I made in a meeting that prevented a problem from happening in the first place. A conversation I had with someone that was quiet and competent and solved something without drama. There's no story there. There's no way to tell it that makes it sound important. And I had to be okay with that. I had to decide that I could matter without an audience."

That's the real shift. Not just the identity change, but the shift in what counts as evidence of mattering. Evidence used to be external. The feedback, the recognition, the emergency call at 2 a.m. that only you could handle. Evidence is now internal. It's the knowledge that you know what you're doing. It's the quiet satisfaction of a thing done well. It's the ability to say no to something and sleep through the night anyway.

The grief includes grieving the loss of that external witness. Because even if the external validation was exhausting, it was also nourishing. It told the person: you matter. You're needed. You're important. The competence-based identity tells the person the same thing, but it tells it quietly, internally, and the person has to listen carefully to hear it.

Many people don't make this transition at all. They age out of the effort-based identity without ever transitioning into the competence-based one. They just get tired and stay tired. They never learn to rest. They never learn to witness themselves. They never learn that they can matter without the adrenaline. They just become exhausted versions of the people they used to be. They become the older employee who's still trying to prove something, still working late hours, still unable to let things go, still looking for crises to justify their presence.

But some people do make it. Some people do the work of grieving the old identity. Some people do learn to witness themselves. Some people do develop a competence-based sense of self that includes what came before but isn't defined by it. And those people become something quieter, something steadier, something that can sustain itself without the constant spike of emergency.

* * *

There's a texture to the competence-based identity that's different from the effort-based one. The effort-based identity is sharp. It has edges. It's responsive, reactive, always ready. The competence-based identity is rounder. It's slower. It can hold things without immediately acting on them. It can look at a problem and say: this is interesting, and it's not mine. It can receive criticism without it becoming a crisis. It can succeed quietly.

And the person becomes rounder too. Not softer, necessarily, but less defended. The constant vigilance can ease. The person can genuinely relax because they've learned, through the nervous system, that the threat was partially imaginary. The crisis will be managed. The work will get done. The person is not solely responsible for everything. And the world doesn't actually end when they rest.

The shoulders drop. The jaw unclenches. The breath deepens. The sleep comes. The body begins to trust that it doesn't have to be ready for emergency all the time. And in that trust, something shifts. A larger self becomes possible. A self that's not defined by struggle. A self that can be moved by beauty without needing it to serve a purpose. A self that can receive without needing to give back immediately. A self that can just be.

But the person has to be willing to grieve to get there. They have to let the old identity die. They have to sit with the loss of it. They have to honor what it did, what it protected them from, what it made possible. And they have to be willing to become someone they don't yet fully recognize. They have to be willing to be invisible. They have to be willing to be whole.

And in that difference—in that willingness to grieve, to transition, to become—something begins to move that had been still. Something that was compressed releases. Something that was defended opens. Something that was always waiting for the next thing gets to rest.

And the person, quieter now, clearer now, more themselves than they've ever been, gets to just breathe.

Chapter Eight

The Collapse of the Old Measuring Stick

The woman who wrote had been using AI to draft client emails for six months. Good ones. Her clients received them—sometimes multiple per week—and read them as coming from her hand, and they did what they were supposed to do. No one sent back messages asking for clarification. No one complained about tone. She knew this was solid work. Still, she could feel something collapsing in her chest when she thought about what she was doing.

"I used to sit with my coffee for an hour," she wrote. "Turning the language over and over. My fingers would get cold. I'd forget to drink the coffee because I was too focused on whether 'we understand' was better than 'we recognize' in that sentence. Now I feed a prompt into the tool and edit for five minutes. How am I any different from the people outsourcing their thinking?"

The question sat in her body like a stone. Not a metaphor she used. A literal description of the weight. She could feel it in her sternum when she opened the tool in the morning.

This is what AI does to people. Not immediately what it replaces—the market will handle that conversation, will handle the disruption and the churn—but what it exposes in real time, in the person using it, watching their own hands move differently than they used to. It accelerates a reckoning that was already underway, one that organizations and individuals both knew was coming but nobody wanted to have while it was still optional. The conversation lives in the body before it lives anywhere else.

* * *

The old measuring stick was never actually measuring what we thought it was. For decades it looked like it was: hours logged, rough drafts produced, obstacles overcome, the visible strain. We confused the artifact of struggle with the source of value. We made a kind of faith out of friction because friction felt like proof that something real was happening, that the work was serious, that it mattered. If it was hard, it was probably worth doing.

Consider the typical work narrative. Someone stays late at the office. Their eyes are tired. Their shoulders ache from hunching forward. They have consumed three cups of coffee and forgotten to eat lunch. And we look at that and think: This person cares. This person is serious. This person is doing important work. We reward the visible struggle. We praise the person who looks most worn down. Exhaustion becomes a proxy for value.

AI didn't create the confusion. It has simply made the confusion impossible to keep pretending doesn't exist.

When someone hands you a completed deliverable that would have required three days of your time and required three minutes of the tool's time, something has to fracture. Either the attachment to hours, or the self-respect. Most people cannot bring themselves to break either one deliberately, so the break happens somewhere else—in their sense of who they are in relation to their own work.

The woman editing those client emails was not lazy. She was not cheating anyone. She was watching the scaffolding of her professional identity collapse in real time and trying to figure out which pieces mattered structurally and which were always just decoration, just the theater we put on to make effort visible. She was holding a mirror up to thirty years of work and asking: Was any of that actually mine?

* * *

There is a distinction that needs stating here, and most conversations about AI seem to skip entirely over it. This distinction matters more than the usual debates about whether the technology is good or bad, whether it represents progress or crisis.

A tool extends what you can do. It takes a task and does it on your behalf, but it does not replace the practice of judgment. When you press a button and the tool produces something, the tool has not thought. It has not chosen. It has not decided that this matters more than that. It has not weighed the consequences. A tool performs tasks. It does not make decisions.

A source is where intention originates. It is the location from which direction emerges. It is what a thing comes from. The source is the consciousness that says: This is what I want to accomplish. This is the problem I am trying to solve. This is what matters here. The source carries responsibility because the source chose the direction.

Responsibility is what determines whether a thing has weight. It answers the question: Who decided this mattered? Who will live with what happens because of this decision? Responsibility is something you carry. It means you cannot shed the consequences of your choices onto someone else, or something else.

When you use a hammer, the structure is clear. The hammer is the tool. You are the source of the intention—you have decided what gets built, where it goes, what shape it takes. You remain responsible for the accuracy of your aim, for whether the thing you build works, for what it will be used for.

When you use AI to draft something, the same structure ought to hold, but people have lost track of it. The tool is the tool. You are the source of intention—the actual question being asked, the real problem needing attention, what this is for. Responsibility for whether what the tool produced is accurate, whether it fits the situation, whether it is ethical, whether it solves what needed solving—that stays with you. It does not transfer to the tool. The tool did not decide to send the email. You did.

But we have been taught to feel that accepting a tool's output is equivalent to surrendering your own thinking. That if you do not personally perform the repetitive labor yourself—if you do not sit at the page moving individual words until your back aches—then you have not done the work. This is where the guilt sharpens. This is where people who are manifestly competent start to feel like frauds.

The confusion is real and human. But it is not evidence of any wrongdoing. It is evidence of a category error, a kind of thought that has gotten its categories mixed up.

Someone uses AI to write a first draft. They then spend an hour in actual judgment about what the draft gets right and what it misses entirely, sometimes catastrophically. They find one paragraph worth keeping and rewrite everything else. They read each sentence aloud to test whether it is honest. They ask: Does this sound like me? Does this say what I mean? In this case, they have been the source. They have exercised responsibility. They have done the thinking work. The tool has done what tools do. But if the person has been taught that value lives in labor—in the hours, the struggle, the visibility of effort—then this person will feel like an impostor even though they have done the actual thinking.

And if they feel fraudulent, they will often become fraudulent. The guilt can flip someone's behavior. They will use the tool without the judgment. They will skip the hard part—the actual thinking—and keep only the speed. They will hand off work they have not thought through. They will sign their name to something they do not understand. This is what guilt can do—it can turn people into the very thing they feared being.

* * *

What does AI remove? The mechanical friction. The repetition. The grinding work of making language move when you do not yet know what you are trying to say. The deep tedium of formatting, restructuring, rewriting the draft seventeen times because the second one is still not quite right and you can feel the difference but cannot yet name it.

The physical sensation matters here. There is a particular kind of fatigue that comes from rewriting the same paragraph fourteen times. Your hands know it. Your eyes know it. You have read those sentences so many times that they have stopped making sense. Your brain stops processing the words and starts only recognizing shapes. And then you push past that fatigue, and something shifts, and suddenly the paragraph works. You felt like you had to earn that moment. The difficulty was the price.

This is genuinely valuable to lose. It frees time. It reduces the accumulation of small failures and the weight of having to refine something imperfectly many times before you can move forward. Your hands can rest. Your eyes can focus. Your mind can go deeper into the actual thinking instead of getting stuck in the mechanical loop.

But AI cannot remove the things that actually matter.

It cannot remove the requirement to know what you are trying to say. It cannot supply the taste that tells you when something is sentimental versus genuine, when you are performing emotion versus actually feeling it. It cannot make judgments about whose problem this is and whether your solution actually solves it or just appears to. It cannot generate the moral weight you carry when you understand that something you write will change how someone thinks about something, and that this is your responsibility.

The tool amplifies the person who is already thinking clearly. It expands them, lets them move faster, gets them closer to their actual thinking without so much interference from the mechanical stuff. It also amplifies the person who is not thinking clearly. It lets them move faster into confused territory. It lets them produce plausible-sounding work without ever clarifying what they are actually trying to do. It generates the appearance of thinking without the substance.

This is the point most people miss when they are asking themselves whether using AI makes them less of a professional, less of a writer, less of a thinker. The labor was never the thing that made anyone valuable. The labor was the container the actual thing lived in. When the container changes, when the labor becomes optional, people panic. They believe the thing has vanished. It has not. It is just visible now without all the scaffolding of effort around it.

Someone who knows how to ask the right question, who has developed the taste to recognize a good answer when they see it, who understands what matters and why—that person becomes more visibly valuable when they use AI, not less. The work that was hidden inside the mechanical labor becomes the only work that is left. The clarity of their thinking shows through without the noise.

Someone who doesn't know any of those things becomes more visibly incompetent. The tool strips away the excuse of effort. There is nowhere to hide.

* * *

There is a moment most people working near AI encounter, and it is worth looking at carefully.

You ask the tool for something. A proposal. A section of analysis. A response to a difficult question. The tool produces something. You read it and think: That is good. That is actually good. I would feel proud if I had written it myself. I would have shown this to colleagues. I would have felt smart.

This is when people panic. Or feel guilty. Or both, guilt layered on panic like sediment.

But this moment is actually information. It is precise information about what the tool can do, and therefore what you cannot outsource if you want the work to be yours.

The tool can produce competent. It can replicate pattern. It can make something that scans as professional because it has learned from a thousand professional examples. It has absorbed style and structure through pattern matching. It knows what competence looks like because it has seen so much of it.

But competence is not judgment. A tool can write clear sentences. A human has to decide whether those clear sentences are saying something true. A human has to ask: Is this accurate? Does it misrepresent anything? Whose interests does it serve? What am I not saying that matters? These are the questions that separate competence from integrity.

The distance between these is not small. It is everything.

Think of taste as the ability to feel whether something is operating at the right frequency for this specific moment, for this specific person, for this specific problem. The tool can mimic resonance. It can produce text that sounds like it is resonating. But it cannot feel whether the resonance is earned or performed, whether it is hollow underneath or solid. Only you can know that, because only you understand what is actually at stake in this particular communication, what the consequences are if you get it wrong, what you know about the person who will read it. You know what their face looks like. You know what they worry about. You know what would land and what would land wrong.

Think of judgment as the ability to hold a question long enough that the answer that emerges is the real answer, not the first answer or the expected answer or the answer that sounds most professional. The tool produces answers instantly. Instantly. But an answer that arrives instantly is almost never the real answer. It is the available answer, the answer that fits the pattern, the answer that the database recognizes. The tool cannot tell the difference. You can, if you practice it, if you know what your actual thinking feels like, if you can distinguish between the moment when you understand something and the moment when you have merely recognized the shape of understanding.

Think of moral weight as the understanding that something you make or say will shape how someone thinks, and that this is a responsibility, and that you cannot avoid it by claiming you were just making something for efficiency. The tool has no capacity for this. It cannot feel weight. It cannot carry consequence. It can produce sentences about responsibility. It can write eloquently about accountability. It cannot bear any of it. You bear it. The moment you sign your name, you bear it.

These three things—taste, judgment, the capacity to feel moral weight—have become harder to dismiss as valuable now that the tool can do everything else. Before, people could argue that writing is just stringing words together. Now that the tool can do the stringing, people have to acknowledge that writing is something else entirely. Writing is deciding what is true. Writing is the responsibility you take for that decision.

* * *

The sober truth is this: AI is an amplifier.

It amplifies the person who knows what they are doing. They use it to extend their reach, to reduce the friction between thinking and making something, to move past the work that does not require their full attention and toward the work that does. Their intentionality becomes clearer. They work faster, but the quality of their judgment does not change. It often improves, because they have more time to actually think, to sit with a problem, to test their first answer against their experience, to let something simmer while they attend to other things.

It also amplifies the person who does not know what they are doing. It lets them produce work that seems competent without having to clarify what they are actually trying to do. It lets them move fast into confused territory and not realize they are confused until someone is relying on their work and their work fails them. They produce plausible-sounding things that crumble under scrutiny. They sound knowledgeable until someone who actually knows asks a follow-up question.

Neither of these outcomes is the fault of the tool. The tool is just showing people how they actually work, at scale and at speed.

The question of whether to use AI is not a question anymore. That answer has already been decided. The tool exists. People are using it. Organizations are reorganizing themselves around it. If you are refusing to engage with it at all, you are making a choice—a deliberate choice, hopefully—about your own professional obsolescence. That is a choice you are allowed to make. You should understand what you are choosing.

The real question is different and harder: Can you use it without abandoning yourself in the process?

Can you use the speed without surrendering the thinking? Can you let the tool do its work without pretending that doing its work is the same as doing your work? Can you edit something with genuine rigor, or will you just accept it because it came out fast and looks good? Can you feel when something is actually solving the problem versus just sounding like it might?

These are not easy questions. They require that you know yourself quite well—that you know what your actual thinking sounds like, how it moves, what texture it has. You need to be able to recognize when you are pretending to know something you do not. You need to feel the difference between clarity and performance, between something that is real and something that is merely plausible. You need to have spent enough time with your own thinking to recognize the difference.

But these are the questions that matter now.

* * *

I knew a woman who worked in corporate communications. She had been doing it for twelve years. She could sit down and write a difficult email to a stakeholder—the kind where you have to deliver bad news without triggering defensiveness, where you have to be honest without being reckless—and she would do it in two drafts. People told her that was impressive.

Then she tried using AI.

She gave it the same problem: Draft an email to the CFO explaining that we need to delay the product launch because we found a structural flaw in our assumptions. The tool produced something in seconds. She read it and felt her stomach drop. It was professional. It was clear. It had all the right components. And it had no actual judgment in it. It did not understand what was at stake for her, for the company, for the CFO's credibility. It did not understand the political terrain. It just understood the form of a difficult communication. The shape of honesty without the substance.

She spent an hour rewriting it. Not because the tool had done a bad job. But because she was the only one who could make the decision about what tone was honest in this particular moment, with this particular person. The tool could give her a starting place. The thinking had to be hers.

She kept using the tool after that, but differently. As a draft engine, a way to get past the blank page. Not as a replacement for the hard part. When she needed to explain difficult things, she still did the work. The tool just helped her skip the part where she was staring at a blank screen.

There is a man I know who is an architect. He has been designing buildings for thirty years. When rendering software became sophisticated enough to show clients what a space would look like in perfect photorealistic detail—not the schematic drawings that used to be the only option, but actual-looking renderings, with light and shadow and texture—something changed for him. He could no longer rely on the client being impressed by the quality of his technical drawings. The drawings were suddenly easy. The tool made them easy.

For about six months this terrified him. He felt like his expertise had vanished, like the thing that made him valuable—the precision of his drawings, the skill it took to render a space convincingly on paper—had been handed to software. He would wake up at three in the morning thinking about obsolescence.

Then it clarified him.

He was still designing exactly as he had always designed: asking the hard questions about what the space needed to do, sitting with the problem until he understood it, making choices based on what was actually required, not what was comfortable. The rendering was just faster now. His thinking did not change. But his thinking became the thing people actually paid for, because the rendering was no longer the bottleneck between his ideas and the client's understanding. The technical skill was still there. It just was no longer the thing anyone was paying for.

That is what is happening to writing, to analysis, to research, to translation, to a dozen kinds of work that require judgment more than they require labor. The labor is being stripped away, and what is left is the thinking, naked and visible.

The people who panic are usually the ones who thought their value was in the labor. The people who get clearer are usually the ones who knew their value was in the thinking all along, and they are just relieved that the proof is finally visible.

Both things are happening right now. In your field. In your specific role. In you.

* * *

To the person who feels guilty about using AI:

Your guilt is not evidence of wrongdoing. This bears repeating because the guilt is usually so loud that it drowns out everything else, makes you defensive, makes you want to prove you are not actually using the tool, or makes you want to use it without thinking as a way to prove that you do not care.

Your guilt is evidence that something in how you understand your own work is in transition. The tools changed. The capabilities changed. You have not caught up yet. You are still living in the old measuring system even though the system itself has been rendered unreliable. That dissonance between the old metric and the new reality is not a character flaw. It is the subject of this entire book.

You might feel like a fraud because you used a tool to draft something. But you are not a fraud for using a tool. You would only be a fraud if you handed off work you did not think through, work you did not take responsibility for, work you did not examine carefully enough to know whether it is good or true or appropriate for the moment.

The question is not whether you used the tool. The question is whether you used it while thinking, or used it instead of thinking.

These are not the same thing and they produce different consequences.

If you drafted something with AI and then spent time in actual judgment—reading what it produced carefully, weighing it against what matters, deciding whether it is true and whether it fits the situation and whether the proportion is right—then you have done your work. The tool shortened the assembly line. You did not shorten the thinking. That is not less. That is actually more visible as thinking, because the mechanical stuff has been stripped away.

If you used the tool and accepted its output without examination, without real judgment, then yes, you made a mistake. But the mistake is not that you used the tool. The mistake is that you used it without holding yourself accountable for the result. The mistake is using it as an excuse to think less, not as a way to think more clearly.

Most guilt about AI is not actually guilt about using a tool. It is guilt about the old effort-value equation finally cracking, and you feeling the vibrations but not yet understanding what is breaking.

* * *

What this means on the ground is specific and unglamorous.

It means asking yourself before you use the tool: What am I actually trying to accomplish? What is the real problem I am trying to solve? If I did not have this tool, what would I have to do, and what would that require of me? These are clarifying questions.

It means using the tool to handle what it handles well—the blank page, the formatting, the pattern work, the things that require recognition of structure—and then doing your own work on top of that.

It means being honest about when you do not know the answer and using the tool to get to a draft that lets you see what you actually think, rather than accepting the draft as your thinking.

It means recognizing that you are now in a world where someone can produce a passable imitation of good work without ever having to do good thinking. That person will not last. Their work will fail in ways that are small at first and catastrophic eventually. But they will exist. They will seem successful for a while. You will have to make peace with that.

It means understanding that your actual value—the thing that cannot be automated—is now the only thing that counts. This is terrifying if you have been relying on the visible labor to feel like value. This is clarifying if you have an actual skill to offer.

It means understanding that ease is not the enemy. Friction was never the virtue. The virtue was always clarity, accuracy, judgment, the capacity to know what matters. The effort was just the environment those things lived in. Now that the environment has changed, those capacities need to be visible on their own.

* * *

The old measuring stick measured effort. It was never actually reliable. It just looked like it was. A person could work very hard and produce something useless. Another person could solve something in an afternoon that seemed like magic. We called the second person talented. We called the first person unlucky. But effort was still the metric we trusted, the thing we could point to.

AI has made it impossible to trust that metric. The tool has stripped away the visible labor, and now the measuring stick is much colder, much more precise, much more accurate. You cannot hide in the hours anymore. The work has to stand on its own.

Can you think clearly? Can you hold a problem long enough to understand it? Can you tell the difference between a real solution and a performance of a solution? Can you live with the consequences of what you make? Can you do it again tomorrow, and the day after? Can you do it when no one is watching?

These are the questions that matter now. The labor was never what they were measuring. It was just very loud, and the loudness made it easy to pretend it was measuring something.

Now it is quiet.

You can hear the questions clearly.

PART III

CREATING WITHOUT SELF-BETRAYAL

Chapter Nine

Authorship Without Punishment

The relief comes quietly. You finish something—a piece of writing, a project, a decision—and instead of immediately fastening yourself to its defense, you simply place it down. Your hands open. You breathe. It is not yours to carry anymore, but it is still yours to answer for. There is a difference, and this difference rewrites everything about how you create.

For years, authorship meant something closer to ownership through suffering. You authored something when you could prove the cost. The longer the nights, the more you questioned yourself, the more you revised past the point of sense—that was when the thing finally belonged to you. Authorship was a claim you earned by bleeding into it. The work was yours because you had paid enough. Enough what? The question never had an answer. Enough was always more than you had already given.

There's a particular texture to this economy, the way it lives in the body. The tight jaw at midnight. The shoulders hunched up around your ears. The weight in your chest that says you should still be working, should still be doubting, should still be revising. You learn to associate creation with a kind of self-flagellation, so that ease begins to feel like cheating. If it didn't hurt to make, then you must not have made it. If you're not exhausted, you're not working. The body becomes a keeping-score machine, measuring your worth in pain units, sleep debt, the number of times you almost quit.

This model is exhaustion wearing a crown.

* * *

What we are moving toward is simpler and harder to trust: authorship as a quiet act of responsibility. Not performance of ownership. Not a manifesto nailed to the door. Not a need to explain every choice, every influence, every moment of doubt. Just: I made this. I directed it. I shaped it with intention. I stand behind what it says. That is authorship. Everything else is theater.

When you stand behind your work without the theater, something shifts in how you move through the world. You are no longer a defendant. You are not building a case for why you deserved to make what you made. There is no jury. There is only clarity about what you chose and why those choices matter to you. Your spine straightens. You stop glancing over your shoulder. You inhabit your own authority without needing to defend it.

A woman I know—let me call her Sarah—spent two years revising an essay collection before realizing she was revising out of fear, not out of fidelity to her own voice. I overheard her explaining this to a friend at a coffee shop, her voice low, almost embarrassed. Each pass made the prose safer, she said. More defended. Less like her. She had internalized the message that good work required suffering—that revision was a kind of punishment, a form of payment. The friend asked what changed. Sarah paused for a long moment, then: "I submitted it when the essays said what I actually believed. Not when they were perfect. When they were true."

I watched her shoulders drop when she said that word. True.

Her entire body shifted with that single syllable. The defensive posture dissolved. She was no longer holding the work away from herself protectively, no longer braced for criticism.

That was when she became the author.

Before that—all that revision, all those nights of sitting in her study with the screen glowing—she had been performing authorship. Playing the role of some-one serious enough, careful enough, wounded enough to deserve to have written something true. The actual authorship was a single decision: "This is what I think. This is what I've seen. I'm willing to stand here and say it." The decision didn't require years. It required a moment. A moment of alignment. Not alignment with some external standard of goodness or acceptability, but alignment between the work and her own deepest knowing.

Notice what wasn't required: proof that she suffered. Visibility of her labor. An explanation of her process. A timeline of her doubt. None of it mattered to the work itself. It mattered only to her need for permission—for evidence that she was allowed to have made something. The approval she was seeking wasn't from readers. It was from some internalized authority, some voice that said good creators earn their right through blood and insomnia. That voice isn't real. It's a story. And stories can be rewritten.

Standing behind your work means you've stopped asking permission. You've moved from the effort economy into the expression economy. In the effort economy, worth is proportional to pain. Your work is valuable because you hurt. Your sleepless nights are your currency. The difficulty is your proof. The more you suffered, the more legitimate your claim to creation. In the expression economy, worth is proportional to alignment. Your work has integrity because you meant it. The effort is irrelevant. The suffering is irrelevant. What matters is whether you made choices and whether you can articulate why those choices matter.

The body experiences this shift as a kind of loosening. The jaw relaxes. You can actually breathe. Your shoulders drop away from your ears. The chronic tension that lived in your upper back for years because you were always carrying something—defending something, proving something—finally releases. It's possible this is the real relief: not the work being done, but the permission you finally grant yourself to stand as you are.

* * *

This is where responsibility enters, and most people misunderstand it completely.

Responsibility does not mean suffering for your work. It does not mean spending sleepless nights worrying about what critics will say. It does not mean over-explaining, over-defending, over-justifying yourself to anyone who questions your right to have made something. Responsibility is not atonement. It is not self-mortification wearing the name of ethics. It is not penance. It is attention.

Responsibility is: Did I actually make this choice, or did I default into it? Am I willing to be accountable for the result? Can I articulate why I made the choices I made? That is the whole thing. Not the performance of responsibility. Not the visible burden. Not the exhaustion you wear like a badge. Just those three questions. Just that basic accounting between you and yourself about what you actually did.

A man I know writes code. For years he felt he had to own every single line—to understand every function, to write everything from first principles, to be able to explain why every variable name existed. I listened to him describe this once, sitting in a conference room between sessions. His hands kept moving as he talked, sketching invisible patterns, as if his body was still trying to write everything from scratch. The idea that he might use a library, or generate code with assistance, or build on someone else's scaffold felt like it would disqualify him from calling himself a programmer. He was drowning in the need to prove authorship through the visibility of his labor. He was drowning in the need to prove he had suffered enough. Every shortcut felt like a kind of fraud.

Then he stopped. He used tools. He built faster. He made choices about what to care about—what he needed to understand completely and what he could rely on others to have solved. The shift didn't happen all at once. He made smaller choices first. He used a library for something he'd previously written by hand. He asked for help on a problem rather than grinding through it alone. Each time he did, he waited for the disqualification to come. It never did. Instead, his work got better.

He became responsible for the architecture, the problem-solving, the decisions about what tools belonged where. He became irresponsible about pretending he had written every character on his own. He became okay with being the person who directed the work, rather than the person who executed every single line. This is what authorship actually means in a world of collaboration and tools and collective knowledge. It's not about doing everything yourself. It's about being intentional about what you do and don't do.

His work got better. And his claim to authorship became unshakeable—not because he could prove how much he suffered, but because he could explain what he chose and why those choices served the problem. He could say: I picked this database because of X. I integrated this library because of Y. I built the core logic myself because of Z. Those were decisions. Those were acts of authorship. He could stand in front of the work and account for it without apology.

Responsibility without martyrdom means you pay attention instead of paying in pain. It means you make deliberate choices and stand behind them. It does not mean you must have done everything with your own hands. It does not mean you must be able to explain how long it took or what process you followed or how many times you failed. Responsibility is about accountability for the result, not advertisement of the effort. The distinction is crucial. When you stop broadcasting the pain, you have room to actually make something. When you stop spending energy on the performance of difficulty, you can spend that energy on the actual work.

When you separate these two things—authorship from suffering, responsibility from visibility—something unexpected happens. The work gets clearer. Your choices become more honest. You stop editing for pain and start editing for clarity. You stop revising to prove you cared and start revising because you actually care about what it says. You can feel the difference in the work itself. It moves differently. It breathes. It stops sounding defensive and starts sounding like someone who knows what they made.

* * *

Integrity is the word people reach for when they're trying to explain this, and then they immediately corrupt it with martyrdom.

Integrity does not require self-sacrifice. This is the lie that has cost artists, writers, makers everything. This is the lie that has kept people from making anything at all, convinced that to create something worthy, they must first destroy themselves. Integrity does not mean cutting away the parts of yourself that make you human. It does not mean suffering in service of purity. It does not mean refusing help because asking would make your claim to authorship less valid. It does not require you to carve away anything. In fact, it requires you to include more, not less.

Integrity is alignment.

It is the alignment between what you actually believe and what you create. It is the alignment between your values and your choices. It is the alignment between the work you release and the person you are. When those three things are aligned—when you create from honest ground and you release it without apology and you can still recognize yourself in it—then the work has integrity. Everything else is performance. And performance, no matter how sophisticated, eventually shows its seams.

A woman I know spent years trying to write a novel that would matter to people who didn't know her. She wanted it to be universal. Big. To rise above the specificity of her own life. I remember her describing this in an interview I read, the way she kept using the word "transcend." She thought that was integrity—that it meant transcending the particular, rising above the mundane details of her own existence to reach something larger. The kitchen where she learned to be afraid. The specific way her father's silence worked. The particular color of the light in the bedroom where she first understood heartbreak. All of it seemed too small, too specific, too much like her. The book stayed stuck. She could not find the story because she was so busy trying to make it not be her story. She was trying to strip away everything specific in service of something grand.

When she finally wrote the thing, it was because she stopped trying to have integrity and started trying to have alignment. She wrote directly from her own life, her own confusion, her own wholly specific moment. She wrote what she had actually seen and felt. She wrote about the way light came through her kitchen window at six in the morning. About the exact cadence of her mother's voice when she was angry. About her own particular failure, the one that only she could have failed, in exactly the way she failed. She did not try to make it mean something bigger. She just let it mean what it meant. She let it be small and true and hers.

Now people who have never met her feel like they know her. Because the work is aligned with who she is. Because she is still recognizable in every sentence. Because she refused to polish away the specific in service of the universal. The universal arrived anyway, not through abstraction but through the depth of her specificity. Because when you write true enough about your own life, it turns out to be everyone's life. The light at six in the morning is everyone's light. The anger in a voice is everyone's anger. The specific failure is every failure.

Integrity does not happen through sacrifice. It happens through honesty. It is the posture of someone who has stopped pretending to be anyone other than themselves. Who has stopped editing for an imagined audience. Who has stopped trying to prove they deserved to create in the first place. That person does not need to suffer to have integrity. They just need to mean it.

* * *

The language matters enormously here. How you speak about your work shapes what you believe about your right to have made it. The words you choose become the structure you live inside. They become the walls of the room you stand in when you present yourself to the world.

For years, when someone asked you about your work, you probably apologized first. You explained the conditions under which you made it—the shortage of time, the limitations of resources, the ways it was less than it could have been. You were accounting for yourself. Justifying. Preparing the ground so that if they did not like it, they would at least understand why it failed. You were asking them in advance to be gentle with something you had already written off as insufficient. You were doing their criticism for them before they had a chance to say anything at all.

That is the language of someone still trying to buy permission. Still trying to explain why someone in your position was allowed to create at all. Still convinced that you need approval from someone else before you're entitled to claim what you made.

The new language is simpler. "This is mine. I made choices. I take responsibility.

I offer it."

Not: "I know it's not perfect, but..."

Not: "I wish I had more time, because then..."

Not: "With better resources, I could have..."

Not: "I did this in between everything else I was supposed to be doing..."

Not: "I'm not really a writer/artist/maker, but..."

Just: "I made this. This is what I think. This is what I see. Take it or leave it."

People often mistake this for arrogance. It is not arrogance. Arrogance is defensive. Arrogance shouts. Arrogance is someone still trying to prove something, still desperate to convince you they're worthy. This is just calmness. The posture of someone who has left the effort economy. Who has stopped needing the other person's permission to have made something. Who is simply standing still, holding their work in open hands, and saying: here. This exists. I made it. I stand behind it. No more, no less.

The body knows the difference. When someone presents their work from a place of defensiveness, you feel it as a kind of tension. They're braced for impact. Their jaw is tight. Their eyes are watching for your reaction. When someone presents their work from a place of calm authority, you feel that instead. They've placed it down. They're not waiting for judgment. They're waiting for you to do whatever you're going to do with it. There's an ease in their shoulders. A steadiness. They've already decided it's real, so they're not worried about convincing you.

That is all authorship has ever been. Everything else is theater.

* * *

There is a new ethics emerging here. It is an ethics of creation without exhaustion. Contribution without over-explanation. Value without the requirement that you prove you deserve it.

The old ethics said: you may create something good if you are willing to suffer for it. If you suffer enough, publicly enough, visibly enough, you earn the right. The suffering is the tax. The exhaustion is the cost of entry. Show us your scars. Show us your all-nighters. Show us how you deprived yourself to make this. Show us the price you paid. Then we will believe your work is worth something. The logic was circular but felt absolutely true: the more it cost you, the more it was worth. The harder it was, the more valid it became.

The new ethics says: you may create something if you stand behind what it says and you made intentional choices in making it. That is the only tax. That is the only cost. Everything else—the hours, the struggle, the visible pain—is irrelevant. Worse than irrelevant. It actually obscures what matters, which is whether you meant it.

This is enormously liberating for some people and enormously unsettling for others. Because for years, the struggle was the proof. The sleepless nights were your ticket. The suffering was how you knew you were doing something real. To be told that you can create something real without the suffering, without the visible pain, without proof of your labor—it can feel like you're being let off the hook. Like there must be some trick. Like you're getting away with something.

You are not getting away with anything. You are just not paying a tax you never owed.

The new ethics makes room for all kinds of creation. The creation that required years of patient work and little visible effort. The creation that happened quickly, cleanly, in flow. The creation that required collaboration, help, tools, scaffolding. The creation that came from struggle, yes, but the struggle that happened years ago, invisible now, integrated into your bone. The creation that came from joy. From curiosity. From the simple question: what would happen if I made this? From play. From the desire to see what your hands could do.

All of this is authorship. All of it is valuable. All of it deserves to exist without the creator having to prove they suffered enough to deserve it. The woman who wrote her novel in three months. The man who code-generated a solution. The person who asked for help and built something better because of that help. The artist who worked for thirty years on the same problem and finally solved it because she could see it differently. The person who made something on a whim and was startled by its beauty. All of it counts. All of it matters.

The cost is just: you have to know what you believe. You have to make choices. You have to stand there and say this is mine. That's all the gate-keeping there is anymore. That's all the permission you need.

* * *

And then there is the question of realness, which people almost always get wrong.

Realness is not something you perform. It is not a tone you strike. It is not about being vulnerable in all the right ways, raw in all the marketable ways, honest about all the approved struggles. The moment it becomes a performance, it has already been lost. You cannot perform genuineness. You can only do the work and let what emerges be what it is.

Most of the people who say they are committed to being real are actually committed to a very particular performance of realness. The performance that looks like: visible struggle, self-disclosure, the appearance of unpolished rawness. That look is not genuine. It is a carefully constructed aesthetic. It is art. It is a style choice, and a savvy one, because that style is currently marketable. People buy unpolished rawness. They pay for intimacy. They reward visibility of pain. The marketplace rewards that particular performance of rawness, so it has multiplied. Everywhere you look, someone is performing it, and because so many people are doing it so well, it starts to feel like the only form of real.

And that is fine. Art is good. Aesthetics matter. Style is not a dirty word. But do not call it realness. Call it what it is: a choice about how to present, a decision about what to reveal and what to keep private, a strategic use of vulnerability for connection. None of these things are bad. But they are not the same as being genuine.

The real thing—the alignment between what you believe and what you make—often requires the least visible struggle. Because the struggle happened years ago. It happened when you were learning your craft, when you were figuring out what you believed, when you were deciding what mattered. By the time you sit down to create, that struggle is integrated. It is in your hands. It is in the choices you make without thinking about them. Your fingers know what to do before your mind catches up. Your ear knows what sounds right. Your eye knows what's balanced. That integration is invisible from the outside, but it's what allows you to move through the work with ease.

A woman I know is a musician. She spent fifteen years studying, practicing, experimenting, failing, learning. She played in living rooms and basements. She took lessons from teachers who pushed her hard, who made her work until her fingers bled, who made her repeat the same phrase a hundred times until she understood what it meant. She made pieces that fell apart. She made pieces that worked. She learned what sound was, how it lived in space, how it could move through a listener's body. Then she started making music that sounded effortless. Clean. Like it arrived almost whole. Like she had simply opened a door and the song walked through, fully formed.

People asked her: how did you make this so easily? What is your secret? How do you access that flow?

She had to explain that the flow was the result of the fifteen years. The ease was earned. The apparent effortlessness was the whole point of all that effort. She had practiced so much that she no longer had to think about the mechanics. Her hands moved without instruction from her conscious mind. Her ear guided her. She could listen to what the piece wanted to become and simply follow it. She could just create from her fullest understanding. The struggle had become invisible because it had become integrated. It lived in her body now. It lived in the thousands of hours that her fingers had learned. It lived in the way her ear had been trained to hear.

That is real. Not the display of struggle. The integration of it.

When you stop trying to perform a certain kind of performance and start making work that is actually aligned with who you are—work you mean, work that reflects what you have learned, work you stand behind without apology—you are not trying to look like something you're not. You are just being yourself. You are just making something that only you could make, in the way that only you would make it, because it comes from the exact specificity of your own life and experience. The work that is hardest to fake is also the work that looks the easiest. Because it comes from a place of such deep knowing that the maker is not performing anymore. They are not trying to look like a creator. They are just creating. And that calmness, that absence of performance, that is what being genuine actually looks like.

* * *

So you finish something. You place it down. Your hands open.

You have stood behind it. You have made deliberate choices. You have taken responsibility for what it says. You have not had to prove you suffered. You have not had to over-explain. You have not had to justify why you made it or how long it took or what tools you used. You have just made it and released it. You do not carry it forward like a weight. You do not keep trying to defend it. It stands on its own, or it doesn't, and either way, you're not accountable for someone else's response. You're only accountable for having meant what you made.

This feels small. It is not small.

You have left the effort economy. You have entered the expression economy. You have moved from a relationship to your work that was based on punishment to one that is based on alignment. You have stopped asking permission to have made something. You have started saying: this is mine. Quietly. Without apology. Without defense. Your body inhabits space differently now. You are no longer braced. You are no longer a defendant. You are no longer trying to prove something that shouldn't need proving.

You are an author.

And that changes everything about how you move through the rest of your work, the rest of your life. Because now you know that your worth does not come from suffering. It comes from meaning what you make. It comes from alignment. It comes from the willingness to stand still and say: I made this. I mean this. I stand behind this. I offer it. And then you release it. Not as a plea. Not as a confession. As a simple fact. As a statement of what exists now because you chose to make it.

That is enough.

It has always been enough.

You just had to stop paying the tax you never owed to finally believe it.

Chapter Ten

Releasing What Drains, Keeping What's Alive

Your shoulders drop when you close the laptop. Not because you finished something good. Because it's over. The meeting was two hours long. You said yes to the revision without checking your calendar first. You smiled at the email about the additional client who heard about you through someone's cousin. Your chest stayed tight the whole time.

This is what drain feels like in the body before it becomes a story you tell yourself.

* * *

Most conversations about quitting or releasing work assume the answer comes first. You decide it's time. You announce it cleanly. You move on. But the people who actually stop doing the work that doesn't serve them rarely experience it that way. They notice first. The noticing comes as small bodily signals that arrive before any reasonable argument for change. A tightness in the throat when you open a particular file. The way you check your phone during work you supposedly love. The sensation of breath becoming shallow the night before a certain meeting. Your hand hesitates over the keyboard for thirty seconds before the cursor moves. Your voice gets smaller in emails to that client. You start drafting responses and deleting them, knowing no words will feel right.

The body speaks first. The rational mind arrives later, offering explanations for what the nervous system already knows.

* * *

Drain is not the same as difficulty. Hard work can nourish. A project that stretches your capacity might leave you tired but also alive. What matters is the direction of the exchange. Drain moves in only one way: out. The work takes more than it returns. You give energy and receive obligation in return. You finish and feel emptier than when you started. This happens consistently, not occasionally. Not every Monday, but every project. Not sometimes, but structurally.

This is the work that keeps asking. Another revision. Another small adjustment. Another client conversation that was supposed to be thirty minutes but sprawls into two hours because they're anxious and you absorb the anxiety. By the time you disconnect from the video call, your jaw is clenched and your stomach is tight. You can feel the tightness for hours afterward. It doesn't fade. It compounds.

Nourishment works differently. The work may be exhausting. Your hands might shake. You might wonder if you're doing it right. But something accumulates. A sense of building. A feeling that the effort itself contains something you needed to discover. You finish depleted in muscles but oddly full elsewhere. Your mind returns to the problem unbidden. You think about it at 10 p.m. without resentment. There's a difference between thinking about work because you must and thinking about it because the problem has become interesting to you. One is obligation. One is curiosity. One leaves a deposit.

The distinction matters because many people leave good work because it's hard, and stay with depleting work because it's easy or familiar or pays well.

* * *

I overheard a conversation at a coffee shop. Two women at the next table, one of them saying: "I kept the job for three more years because I felt like I couldn't leave. Like it would mean the whole thing was a mistake."

Her friend leaned forward. "Was it?"

"No. It was fine. The money was fine. The people were fine. But I was just... managing. Getting through. My shoulders never relaxed. I'd spend my weekends recovering from my own job."

The first woman had been a consultant. She'd built her practice around solving operational problems for nonprofits. It paid well. It was useful. Nobody argued with her choice. The work had become completely automatic. She could walk into an organization's chaos, diagnose the systems problem in two hours, deliver a report, and collect a check. She no longer had to think during the process itself. This efficiency was a superpower on paper. In her body, it felt like disappearing.

She started noticing how she scheduled her actual writing—the essays she wanted to publish—for Wednesday afternoons, a slot she rarely protected. How the consulting projects always expanded, gently pushing into that time. How she kept the consulting rate high enough that she could "afford" to do writing eventually. Eventually kept moving further away. She had conversations with herself about discipline. She bought better writing software. She read books about productivity. The books didn't help because the problem wasn't her system. It was her energy. The consulting work was feeding itself first.

She'd sit down to write on Wednesday afternoons with the consulting project done, but her mind would still be there, still arranging the pieces. She'd write a paragraph. Delete it. Write another. Delete that. Nothing felt true. The writing tasted like obligation because it was being done in the leftover hours. The work wasn't getting her actual attention. It was getting her good intentions.

* * *

What happened next was not dramatic resignation. She didn't quit. She simply stopped pitching.

When existing clients called, she didn't reject them, but she didn't actively search for new ones. The momentum of the work naturally slowed. She sent fewer emails. She declined new opportunities. Within six months, three major projects ended simultaneously. One client decided to hire someone in-house. Another company restructured. The third found a different consultant. The endings came without her having to announce anything. She'd stopped feeding the machine, and the machine, as it turned out, depended entirely on her feeding it.

She was terrified for about three weeks. The bank account stopped moving. Her email stayed quiet. She found herself obsessively checking for messages that didn't arrive. She wondered if she'd made a terrible mistake. What if nobody called back? What if she'd burned bridges? What if the writing still didn't happen?

Then something unexpected arrived. Not confidence. Something quieter than that. A recognition. The panic subsided and she realized she'd been waiting for permission that was never coming. The work wasn't going to release her. She had to release it. No one else was going to decide that her time was too valuable for the work that didn't matter. No client was going to suggest she focus on her real interests. No one had the authority to give her that permission. She had to take it.

The distinction here is important. She didn't quit. She didn't make a decision and announce a new chapter. She simply stopped feeding the machine. Without her active effort to sustain it, it slowly starved. The clients didn't disappear—they'd found other solutions. But the work didn't remain available for her to return to at some future date when she had more time. It moved on. It became someone else's work.

I asked her later: "Were you afraid it would all collapse?"

"Terrified," she said. "But that's not what happened. The consulting work didn't collapse. My clients solved their problems. They found people who wanted to do it. I was the one who was collapsing, slowly, and nobody was going to notice but me."

* * *

Strategy asks one question: "What should I do?"

It produces spreadsheets, timelines, quarterly goals, metrics. Strategy is useful when you're building something with other people and you need to coordinate effort. It's useful when the desired outcome is clear and measurable. But strategy assumes the plan knows more than you do. Strategy says the future is knowable, that clarity comes from thinking hard enough, that the right answer exists in advance of living.

Activation asks a different question: "What is already alive in me?"

It doesn't produce plans. It produces noticing. A client reached out last Tuesday. A conversation about a topic you'd stopped researching five years ago suddenly matters again. The small project that wasn't on the quarterly goals somehow generated an idea you've been sitting with for months. The person you met once at a conference keeps appearing in your thinking. These aren't major events. They're small tugs. Most people dismiss them as distraction.

Strategy says: Get clarity on the goal. Reverse engineer the path. Execute the plan.

Activation says: Notice where the energy is. There's information there.

Most people have learned to ignore activation in favor of strategy. A goal sounds more responsible. Following an impulse sounds indulgent. Following an impulse sounds like the beginning of failure. But watch what actually happens when someone does follow activation instead. The research deepens because it's interesting, not because they scheduled research time. The writing gets done at 10 p.m. not because it's efficient, but because not writing would feel like resistance. The work doesn't require motivation because it's already moving. The motivation is built in. It's what the nervous system wants.

This isn't about pursuing pleasure. Activation includes work that feels necessary. It includes things that matter even when they're hard. What makes them different from drain is that the difficulty contains something you're drawn toward, not driven away from. The difficulty becomes information. It tells you something about what the work requires. It doesn't tell you to stop.

The consultant started noticing what activated her. It wasn't the operational problem-solving. That had become a perfectly executed pattern. She could do it in her sleep. What activated her was working with founders in the impossible space between vision and viability. Organizations that didn't yet know what they wanted to be. That space felt alive to her. It was unclear. It required discovery. It required her to actually think instead of deploy existing answers.

She started taking on smaller projects with younger nonprofits. The pay dropped.

The problem couldn't be diagnosed in two hours. She didn't have a formula. She actually had to stay in relationship with the uncertainty of what the organization needed. The work became harder and the drain stopped. What had changed wasn't the difficulty level. It was what the difficulty was attached to. One kind of difficulty came with the sensation of giving without return. The other kind came with the sensation of building something she wanted to understand.

She told me: "When I was doing operational consulting, I felt efficient. I felt skilled. But I didn't feel present. With the nonprofit work, I feel like I'm actually there. I'm actually thinking. My brain isn't on some other timeline. I'm not waiting for this to be done so I can do something else."

That's the difference. Drain happens when part of you is already elsewhere.

* * *

Not all signals are equal. Some activation is distraction. Some is avoidance in a pretty costume.

The distinction isn't moral. It's textural. Real activation returns something to you. A pull toward work that matters. Curiosity that persists across time. The kind of interest that doesn't require you to convince yourself. When you notice it, something in you says yes before your mind catches up.

Distraction disguises itself as activation. It's the impulse to start something new because the current work got hard. The appeal of an opportunity that's flattering but doesn't actually align with what you're building. The sudden urgency around a trend that has nothing to do with your own development. The shiny project that promises to make everything finally work. These all feel like pulls. But they're typically pulls away from something difficult, not toward something true. They're escape hatches dressed up as opportunities.

The body knows the difference. Real activation includes steady energy. You return to it. The initial excitement doesn't collapse into obligation. Distraction, by contrast, arrives with a spike. It consumes attention totally for a period. Then it flatlines and leaves you confused about why you were ever interested. You check in with the work two weeks later and feel nothing. The urgency has evaporated. What felt vital is now just another tab open in your browser.

Watch long enough and the pattern shows itself. The work you keep returning to without deciding to. The topics you research without anyone assigning them. The conversations you find yourself having unbidden. The problems you can't stop thinking about. These are directions. They're your system pointing you somewhere.

What if the plan is wrong and the signals are right?

Most people reorganize their lives around a predetermined goal, then wonder why the work that's supposed to be fulfilling feels prescribed. The goal was supposed to be the answer. The goal was supposed to settle things. But a goal is just a guess about what will matter. Your own activation is information from someone who actually knows you—your own future self, whispering back through your nervous system.

She had set out to be an operational systems expert. She'd made that decision at some point. It made sense. It was respectable. It paid well. She built her entire professional identity around it. But over five years, something had shifted. The work no longer spoke to something in her. The signals were pointing elsewhere. She spent a lot of time ignoring them because ignoring them meant not having to rebuild everything.

But rebuilding didn't happen in an afternoon. It happened in the six months where she stopped feeding the old work and started noticing what was pulling her. She kept taking smaller projects. She wrote more. She started having different conversations. She became someone different not because she decided to, but because she spent time paying attention to what was alive.

This doesn't mean you can't have intentions. It means your intentions should inform where you place attention, not replace it. You can want to write a book and also notice what kinds of writing activate you most. You can build a practice and also pay attention to which aspects feel alive versus obligatory. The plan and the signals don't have to conflict if you treat the signals as real data instead of noise.

* * *

Money doesn't arrive with the meaningful work.

This is one of the cruelest realities and also one that most people misread. They assume it means the meaningful work is frivolous. They assume it means they should wait for more financial stability before pursuing what actually matters. They assume the lack of immediate payment is evidence that the work shouldn't exist. They use it as permission to stay with the depleting work. At least it pays. At least it's stable.

What it actually means is that meaning and money operate on different timelines. Meaning builds slowly. It accumulates through consistency, through sustained attention to problems that matter, through work that serves something beyond your own survival. Money, when it comes to that work, arrives later. It arrives because the work became real. Because other people began to depend on it. Because it proved itself first through its own necessity, not through financial validation.

The consultant's pay dropped when she changed her focus. For eight months it was significantly lower. Not catastrophically lower, but noticeably lower. She had savings. She'd built financial margin when the work was easier. That margin was the actual difference between having a choice and being forced back into work that didn't matter. That margin gave her the real freedom to follow what was alive. Not a metaphorical freedom. A real one. Money in an account that said: you can afford to take the work seriously even if it doesn't pay immediately.

This is why the hustle narrative is so seductive and so wrong. Hustle says you should work the depleting job to fund the meaningful work. Work the thing that doesn't matter to build capital for the thing that does. It sounds logical. It sounds like adulting. It sounds like you're being responsible about your dreams. But energy spent on depletion is unavailable for creation. The meaningful work doesn't get your best thinking. It gets your scraps. It gets the leftover moments at 10 p.m. when you're already tired. And it stays scraps because you haven't actually committed resources to it.

There's a different logic. Do enough of the meaningful work to know it's real. Let it inform where you place resources. Let the signals guide the strategy instead of the other way around. Some of that work will need to be funded by other work—work you don't hate but don't love. The difference is intention. That other work is a resource, not the plan. It's temporary, not permanent. It's kept in its place instead of colonizing your entire effort.

The consultant restructured. She kept one ongoing client—smaller scope, predictable monthly income, work that was useful but not alive. Everything else went to the work with founders. The consulting work funded the real exploration. The funding made the exploration sustainable instead of desperate. She wasn't choosing between security and meaning. She was using security to make meaning possible.

* * *

Sustainability is not glamorous.

It doesn't produce inspiration quotes. It doesn't feel important in the moment. It's the opposite of the urgency high that so many confuse with importance. Urgency produces adrenaline. Adrenaline feels like significance. It feels like everything matters. It feels like you matter. When the adrenaline spike comes down, the work feels hollow because what felt important was actually just the biochemistry of panic. You were addicted to the rush, not committed to the work.

Sustainability produces consistency. It feels like nothing. You write a page. You do the work. You stop. You do it again tomorrow. The page doesn't feel momentous. The work doesn't announce itself. Nothing is on fire. Nothing is urgent. You just keep showing up and the book accumulates. A page becomes ten pages becomes a chapter. The accumulation is so slow you might not notice it's happening.

Urgency is the drug that keeps people from their own work. It's the emergency meeting that derails the morning. It's the client crisis that becomes the reason you never started the project. It's the feeling that the nonprofit's survival depends on your immediate response, so the writing has to wait. It's the belief that if you don't solve this right now, everything will collapse. And the collapsed thing you're preventing is always just vague enough that you can't actually examine it. Emergency. Crisis. Urgent. These words close down thinking.

Some urgencies are real. Some genuinely require immediate response. A child is in danger. A building is burning. A medical emergency. These exist. But most of what claims to be urgent is manufactured. It's produced by other people's panic. By the way organizations are structured to confuse busyness with purpose. By the story that maturity means being available for every demand. By people who learned long ago that urgency gets responses, so they code everything as urgent.

Sustainability requires saying no to urgency on behalf of what's alive. This isn't selfish. It's honest. The book won't write itself in the margins. The practice won't build from stolen moments. The work that actually matters requires you to show up regularly, not brilliantly. Consistency beats intensity. A reliable daily practice beats the occasional heroic effort.

The consultant stopped taking emergency consulting calls. She offered a fixed number of hours per month. When those hours were used, she was unavailable. She had a voicemail that said so. She didn't answer emails about additional work. This sounded impossible to her clients at first. Some of them panicked. Some found other people. Some restructured their problems to fit within the available time. What she learned was that most urgency collapses when you're actually unavailable. It was never as critical as it felt. It just felt that way when you were treating it as critical. When you stopped treating it as critical, it found another level. The problem was still there, but it didn't require her anymore.

Her writing time became non-negotiable. Not because it was more important—though it was—but because the book only existed if she wrote it. The consulting clients would find solutions with or without her. They had before she came along. They would again. The book would not exist without her showing up.

* * *

Some work simply dies when you stop feeding it.

This is not failure. This is ecology. Energy is finite. The attention you give to something else is attention withheld from what you're doing now. Growth happens in some directions and not others because you're placing resources in those directions. When you stop, the unmaintained work doesn't transform into something better. It just stops. It gets reclaimed by whatever comes next.

This sounds obvious but it's surprisingly hard to accept. People keep projects alive for years past their usefulness because closing them feels like admitting they were wrong. They sustain roles they've outgrown because the role has momentum and stopping requires action. They maintain relationships with clients who drain them because abandonment feels worse than slow death. There's a guilty relief in not deciding, in letting things quietly stagnate instead of making a choice and having to own it.

But the resources are real. The time is real. The attention is real. Every hour spent on what's already dying is an hour not spent on what's trying to be born. This is the actual cost. Not the guilt. Not the sense of obligation. The real opportunity cost in attention and effort.

The consultant had built a reputation in operational systems work. Her website said it. Her referrals came from it. Closing that door meant her professional identity would shift. She wouldn't be the expert anymore. She'd be someone figuring it out. This felt destabilizing. She'd spent years becoming the expert. And now she'd have to become a beginner at something else.

But the work with founders didn't have space to develop while the operational work was still generating income and reputation. She couldn't be fully invested in both. One was feeding her and her bank account. One was feeding her sense of what she should be doing. She chose to stop feeding the second. She let it die.

It took about a year for the work with founders to generate real income. A year of smaller checks and doubt. A year of wondering if she'd made a terrible mistake. A year of conversations with friends who reminded her of her previous success and asked what she was doing now. A year of updating her LinkedIn and then not updating it because she didn't know what to put. But during that year, she built something that actually mattered to her. She learned things. She made discoveries. She became someone different—not because she decided to, but because she spent a year paying attention to what was alive.

The operational work is still available if she wants it. The skills are still there. The reputation didn't completely evaporate. But she doesn't have to do it because she stopped feeding it. She stopped being the person who solves those problems because she became someone solving different ones. The identity died because she didn't maintain it. And she let it die because something else was trying to live.

* * *

Releasing work is quieter than it sounds.

It doesn't require a resignation letter or an announcement. It requires attention. What are you still doing that you're no longer feeding? What role are you still performing? What client are you still accommodating out of habit rather than choice? What project are you maintaining out of obligation?

Start there. Not with a decision. With noticing. Where does your energy go? Where could it go if those other things stopped consuming it?

The pulling back is often gradual. The client who calls every week gradually calls every other week because you've stopped initiating contact. The project that seemed urgent gradually stalls because you're not pushing it forward. The role you performed becomes harder to sustain because you're not fully present in it anymore. Your interest simply dries up. It's not dramatic. It's the slow evaporation of momentum.

This is not unkind. It's honest. People can generally sense when you're no longer invested. They feel it in how you respond to emails. They hear it in the tone of your voice on calls. Some feel relieved. Some find other solutions or other people. The work finds its level.

What remains is what you're actually feeding. The people you return calls from immediately. The work you think about unbidden. The problems you can't stop solving because they matter to you, not because you're obligated. The projects that have you checking them at 10 p.m., not because you feel you should, but because you want to know what happens next.

This is the ecology of a sustainable creative life. You can't do everything that's possible. You can't serve everyone who asks. You can't maintain work that doesn't nourish you alongside work that does. Energy is the limiting factor. Where you place it determines what grows. What you feed grows. What you starve dies. That's not harsh. That's how life works.

The body knows this already. It's been telling you which work drains and which nourishes. It's been showing you the signals. It's been whispering about what's already dying. The only question is whether you'll listen.

Some people don't. They keep feeding until they're depleted. They perform roles until something breaks. They sustain work until they can't anymore. The crisis comes from the outside—a burnout, a physical illness, a collapse—and that crisis finally gives them permission to stop. The body had been asking for years. It just took a crisis to make the asking loud enough that they couldn't ignore it anymore.

But some people notice earlier. They feel the difference in their chest. They see how they move differently toward different work. They hear how their voice changes. They trust what their own system is telling them about what feeds it and what doesn't. They release quietly. They stop forcing what wants to die. They keep feeding what's alive. And in the space created by that simple ecology, something actually grows.

Chapter Eleven

After Effort

Your shoulders drop two inches the moment you stop proving something. You'll notice this when you're alone, maybe at your desk, and you reach for a piece of work that doesn't need witnessing. The exhale comes first. Then the actual work—smaller, steadier, aimed at something other than evidence. It's the kind of work that can happen in silence, that doesn't require an audience to be valid.

This is who you are when struggle is no longer your credential.

You are not transformed. The word implies a shedding of skin, an emergence from chrysalis into something unrecognizable. You're the same person who fought, who pushed, who wove your legitimacy from blood and sleeplessness. But the math has changed. The equation that once read *pain equals proof* has been crossed out. What remains underneath looks almost ordinary: a person who works because the work asks to be done. Not because not-working would mean erasure. Not because your body is the collateral.

The recognition arrives not in epiphany but in accumulation. In a meeting where you say no without the apologetic second sentence that used to follow. In a manuscript where you cut the sentence that tried too hard, that reached for effect instead of clarity. In the way you listen now—not waiting for your turn to demonstrate how much you've suffered to earn the right to be heard, but actually hearing what's being said. You notice you're no longer cataloging your pain for later proof. The person who emerges from this transition is not more impressive. She is more present. He is less interested in the narrative of his own effort and more interested in what the effort was supposed to build. They see what was always underneath the struggle: the work was never the point. Coherence was.

What disappears first is the suffering tax—that strange currency you learned to trade in, that poisoned exchange rate where agony bought you legitimacy. Every ache became an asset. Every sleepless night a down payment on worthiness. The crushing schedule proved you mattered. The constant state of barely-making-it demonstrated your commitment. You had become fluent in crisis. You spoke it with your body—the clenched jaw, the tight chest, the way your fingers typed faster when anxiety coursed through you. Crisis had become the only language that sounded like love, the only proof that you cared enough.

When you stop speaking it, the silence is disorienting. There's nothing to show for the hour except the hour itself. No red eyes to display. No tremor in your voice from exhaustion. No dark circles to announce your commitment. The silence feels like theft at first. Like you're getting away with something.

This is the strangest part of the transition: learning to trust that rest is not laziness. That a full night's sleep doesn't mean you don't care. That showing up rested doesn't diminish your dedication—it concentrates it. The body forgets this slowly. Your neck muscles still hold tension that no longer has a reason. Your shoulders still creep toward your ears in meetings. Your jaw still clenches on Sunday nights even when there's no emergency. The nervous system was trained in crisis for so long that ease feels like a setup for disaster. You wait for the consequence of not-performing. It comes more slowly than expected, which makes you more suspicious, not less.

* * *

A woman I know—a designer who spent fifteen years building a practice on the scaffolding of her own exhaustion—sits in a coffee shop describing this. Her coffee steams in front of her untouched. "I realized I was working so hard to prove I deserved to work," she says. "Like the work itself wasn't enough. Like I had to suffer to justify taking up space with what I made." She'd been designing while also managing the narrative of her own sacrifice. The subtext was everywhere: the late nights mentioned casually, the missed dinners, the way she'd emphasize how little sleep she was running on. Every client meeting carried a unspoken plea: *See how much this costs me? That's how much I care.*

She describes the shift in her body first. A softening in her shoulders during presentations. Her hands no longer shaking when she sent work. Her voice less defensive, more direct. The vigilance in her chest finally lay down.

One day she submitted a project she'd completed in a reasonable number of hours, with actual rest between starting and finishing. She'd slept eight hours the night before sending it. No crisis. No last-minute revisions born of panic. The work was cleaner for it. The client barely noticed the difference in technical execution, but they responded differently. They trusted it more. Not because it was technically superior—in some ways the earlier version had more of that frenetic polish that comes from desperation—but because this version didn't carry the stench of self-flagellation.

The client asked for fewer revisions. They asked for her input more directly. They didn't seem to feel the need to manage her suffering. The work itself had changed tone because the person making it had.

* * *

What remains when work stops hurting is the actual craft. The irreducible skills. The knowledge of how a form should breathe. The instinct that tells you a narrative is sagging three pages in, that something in the structure is asking for air. The ear for language that can't be faked. The hand that knows how a tool feels, knows the weight of it, the resistance it offers. The judgment that costs nothing to develop but everything to degrade.

Craft doesn't require suffering to be legitimate. It never did. This is one of the lies that persists longest. That pain is the price of excellence. That you have to damage yourself to create something real. Craft is built through repetition, attention, failure, adjustment, and the kind of time that has nothing to do with crisis. A sculptor's hands know the particular resistance of marble because she's touched it ten thousand times, not because she's deprived herself of sleep while touching it. A developer's code is elegant because they've written it poorly five hundred times before, not because they've written it while panicked. The discipline that builds craft is a different animal than the desperation that passed for discipline during your effort years.

What also remains is curiosity—the kind that has nothing to do with ambition. Not the curiosity that asks *How can I do this better than them?* but the curiosity that asks *How does this thing actually work?* There's a specific quality to this kind of wondering. It has no finish line. A potter who spends forty years working with clay doesn't arrive at a point where clay has nothing left to teach. The clay keeps teaching. The glazes shift. The temperature variations become more interesting, not less. A writer doesn't exhaust the possibilities of language. The possibilities multiply. A therapist doesn't run out of human complexity to understand. Each person who walks into the room brings a constellation of contradictions that can't be solved, only recognized. The work doesn't become easier because you've mastered it. It becomes different because mastery teaches you how much you still don't know. This shift—from the frantic proving of the effort years to the steady inquiry of the after—changes the way you move through your own work.

The other thing that remains is the ability to sit with a real question until a real answer surfaces. Not the first answer. Not the answer that sounds good in a pitch or looks impressive in a portfolio. The real one. The one that required you to be quiet long enough to hear it, that couldn't emerge until you stopped generating noise to cover up your doubt. This capacity feels rare because it is. Most people have learned to fill the silence with something—busyness, output, the performance of thought, the constant typing that masquerades as creation. Actual thinking is slower. It can't be optimized. It requires stopping, sitting, tolerating the discomfort of not-knowing long enough for knowing to actually arrive.

When you stop, something happens that no amount of effort can manufacture: clarity. Not the forced clarity of someone who's decided they know something, who's gripped an answer and won't let go. But the clear-eyed witnessing of what is actually there. What works. What doesn't. What's yours to do and what isn't. What you care about and what you were only pretending to care about because other people's investment in your struggle felt like belonging. Clarity is cold in a way that effort's heat obscured. It shows you what's real and what's been performance.

* * *

The work you do after effort is oriented differently. It is oriented toward coherence. Not perfection—coherence. The difference matters so much that it's worth sitting with.

Perfection is a direction. It is infinite, comparative, and aimed outward. It tells you that you are not enough in your current state. It is always receding, always one more revision away, one more accomplishment away, one more sacrifice away. It is the insatiable direction. Coherence is an alignment. It is finite, personal, and aimed at integration. It tells you that your values, your energy, and your output are pointing the same direction. That what you make comes from where you actually stand, not from where you think you should stand, not from where someone else thinks you should stand.

Coherence is what readers feel when they trust a writer. It's not the absence of mistakes or the presence of stylistic perfection. Anyone can learn sentence construction. You can be technically flawless and still sound like you're lying. Coherence is the sense that the person writing actually believes what they're saying. That they're not performing expertise or concern or knowledge they don't have. They've done the work of figuring out what they actually think, and they're telling you that, and the truth of that arrangement is unmistakable. You feel it in your body before you can articulate it. A tightening in the chest that says: this person is not lying. This person knows what they're talking about because they've lived it, not just read about it.

A therapist who works from coherence doesn't follow a script, even an excellent script. She has integrated the training into her actual way of being. The technique is no longer separate from her, held in one hand while she performs something else with the other. It's not something she performs; it's something she inhabits. The client feels this distinction immediately. They trust her not because she knows the right thing to say but because her presence carries the weight of actual understanding. She's been where doubt lives. She's learned how to sit with not-knowing. Her certainty about uncertainty is the thing that heals. It gives them permission to stop pretending to have answers.

A craftsperson working from coherence—a carpenter, a musician, a baker—stops looking for permission. The work is authorized by its own integrity. The dovetail is tight because a loose one would be a lie, would say to the person who opens that drawer: I didn't care enough to get this right. The note is held because cutting it short would betray the phrase, would collapse something the composer built. The bread is allowed to rise until it's ready, not until the schedule says it should be done. No forcing. No performance. This kind of work has a specific gravity. It costs less to make and means more when you receive it because nothing about it was wasted. Nothing was performed for an audience that isn't in the room.

Creating from coherence feels nothing like what you were told creation should feel like. There's no crisis. No racing against time to make the deadline feel urgent, to make the result feel earned through suffering. There's no external pressure manufactured to simulate importance. The importance is intrinsic. The work matters because it will help someone find themselves. Because it will clarify something that was unclear. Because it will make something possible that wasn't possible before. Not because you've suffered to create it.

This is the hardest thing to believe when you're transitioning. That coherent work is enough. That work done from alignment, rather than from desperation, is actually more reliable. That the client, the reader, the listener doesn't need your suffering to validate their trust. They need your presence. They need to know you're actually here, not performing here. They need to sense that you see them and that what you've made is for them specifically, not for the abstract audience you've invented to justify the price of your effort. And they can tell. The body always tells. They'll feel the difference between being served and being used.

The evidence of this is everywhere if you look. The best teachers you've had were not the ones visibly destroying themselves. The artists whose work moved you were not necessarily the most traumatized. The practitioners you return to are the ones who seem to actually know something, not the ones broadcasting how hard they're working to know it. The ones whose presence makes you feel calmer, steadier, more capable. You've always recognized coherence. You're just finally allowed to create it.

* * *

Success, in the old model, was a thing you accumulated through visible effort and external validation. The more impressive the struggle, the more legitimate the success. A book deal meant something because you'd sacrificed for it. A promotion meant something because you'd made yourself indispensable through relentless availability. Money meant something because it was what you'd purchased with your health, with your relationships, with the small deaths of your own joy. The evidence of your value was written on your body as exhaustion and on your calendar as unavailability. Your success could be read in your thinness, your gray hair, the way you couldn't sit still even on vacation because the anxiety of not-producing had calcified into your nervous system.

This model is collapsing—not because it was wrong, but because it was expensive in ways that only become clear when you stop paying.

The new definition of success is stranger because it's not measured in units. It's measured in alignment. Internal alignment: are your actions reflecting your actual values, or are you still performing an older version of your priorities? Are you saying yes to things because they matter or because you're afraid of disappearing? External orientation: does the work help people find themselves? Does it clarify what was confusing? Does it open a door instead of closing one? Does it leave people feeling smaller or larger?

Success in this model looks quiet. It looks like a client who comes back not because they need you to save them, but because you've taught them something about their own capacity. It looks like a reader who writes to say your work helped them understand something about themselves they couldn't articulate before. It looks like the deep breath you take after finishing something because the thing is done and it's sound and you can let it go. Not because you've exhausted yourself making it, but because you've been present enough to make it right. It looks like the ability to rest without guilt, to close the computer and know that the work is held safely, that you don't have to be vigilant against its failure.

This is almost incomprehensible to someone still inside the old model. How can success be quiet? How can it lack the externality that proves it happened? But the paradox is that the quiet work travels further. The coherent work spreads without marketing. The thing made from alignment finds the people it's meant for, not because you've aggressively publicized your suffering, but because the work itself carries a frequency that draws its people toward it. The absence of desperation is its own kind of magnetism.

You can feel this shift happening in your own life if you pay attention. The projects you're most proud of are rarely the ones that required the most obvious suffering. They're the ones where you somehow found the right approach and it held. Where you knew what to do and you did it. Where the obstacles made sense and you solved them rather than being destroyed by them. Where you could actually sleep while the work was underway. Those are the projects that matter. Those are the ones people point to. Those are the ones that have staying power. Not because they're famous or highly rewarded, but because they're real. They carry you in them, not your desperation.

The success you're allowed to have now is success measured by internal coherence and genuine helpfulness. Not by how much you've given up to have it. Not by whether your sacrifice was visible enough to convince people you deserved it. That should be a relief. It usually feels like a loss first.

* * *

Everything that came before—all those years of effort, the struggle that became your signature, the pain that proved your commitment—none of it was wasted. It was training. It was curriculum disguised as crisis.

The effort built capacity. The struggle taught you what you're capable of. The suffering revealed what matters and what doesn't. You learned discernment in those years, learned it through your body, learned it by burning hot enough to see what was combustible and what was durable. You learned the difference between urgency and importance, between busy and productive, between the feeling of working and the feeling of creating something real. You paid in effort so that you could learn what effort is actually for. You burned through your reserves so that you could understand what's essential and what's ornament.

The years you spent in crisis became the foundation for recognizing non-crisis. You can't appreciate ease without having known difficulty. You can't identify coherence until you've experienced what misalignment feels like, until you've felt the friction of being at odds with yourself. Your struggle was not pointless. It was the curriculum. Every lesson cost something, but you were learning what you'd need to know to survive what comes next.

But carrying it forward as an identity is different than learning from it.

Some of what you built in those years is worth keeping: the discipline, the refusal to accept mediocrity, the ability to focus when focus is needed, the skill of turning a deadline into an organizing principle that makes the infinite finite. Some of it is worth releasing: the belief that your value is proportional to your suffering, the performance of crisis, the habit of making yourself small enough to fit in other people's expectations, the strange pride in being too busy to be fully human.

A writer I know spent twenty years working in crisis mode. Deadline-driven. Comparison-fueled. Every piece of writing was a battle in a larger war against obscurity. She'd internalized the idea that real writing had to hurt, that if it wasn't extracted from her like blood she hadn't done it right. Then one day she got sick—not metaphorically, but actually sick. The kind of sick where working twelve hours a day becomes physically impossible. Where your body simply stops cooperating with your ambition. She had six months of enforced rest, and during that time a quiet thing happened. She finished a book. Not because she wrote more. Because she wrote better. Because the pressure cooker had been turned off and she could hear what she actually wanted to say underneath all the noise of what she thought she was supposed to say. The market wasn't screaming at her. Her inner critic had to retreat when her immune system collapsed. What emerged was simpler and more true.

When she recovered, she didn't go back to the crisis model. She'd tasted what it felt like to create without the suffering tax, and the work was too good to abandon. The words came faster when she wasn't moving them against resistance. She'd been so busy proving she deserved to write that she'd never checked whether the suffering was making her a better writer or just more visible.

But she didn't abandon the discipline either. She kept the capacity for sustained focus. She kept the non-negotiable standards. She released the performance of emergency that had become her way of being. The result was a body of work that felt both solid and sustainable. The books didn't sell better, but they sold steadier. They found their people. They stayed in print. They moved people not because the author had suffered, but because she'd actually meant what she wrote.

The difference between writing from desperation and writing from conviction is unmistakable once you've felt it. One is a plea. The other is a conversation. One requires suffering to justify it. The other knows its justification lives in what it says.

This is what the integration looks like. Not going back to the old way, not swinging too far in the opposite direction and becoming passive or checked out. Not deciding that effort itself was the mistake, that ambition was the problem. But finding the third point: the effort that's required without the suffering that's optional. The rigor without the self-destruction. The commitment without the immolation. The professional without the martyr.

* * *

You are not after effort because you failed at effort. You are not arriving here defeated, dragging yourself toward a diminished version of accomplishment. You didn't collapse into this place from exhaustion and decide to make the best of it. You are after effort because you completed it. You have run that race and finished it and found what it had to teach. The struggle was not a door you were locked behind. It was a corridor. You've walked it. You've seen what's at the end. You've touched the other side.

What you've learned in those rooms—the ones made of crisis and self-doubt and the certainty that you had to break yourself to be worth something—that knowledge is real. It's yours. It's earned in a way that can't be taken from you. You can carry it forward not as a burden but as experience. As evidence of what you survived and what you're no longer willing to survive. You know now what it costs. You know what you're worth.

The work is different now. Not because you gave up. Because you arrived.

You arrive at a place where your word is already good. People trust you not because you've performed urgency but because you've delivered quality consistently. You no longer apologize for saying what you mean. You can say no without story, without crisis. The no lands cleanly.

Rest isn't a betrayal but a requirement. You take it without the burden of guilt. The work comes from fullness rather than depletion. You show up with something in the tank. Your hands aren't shaking from coffee and desperation. And somehow that makes the work better. More inventive. More generous. More able to meet people where they actually are.

The person working after effort is recognizable by specific qualities. She moves without the constant forward-lean, without the tension of someone always bracing for the next disaster. You can see it in the way her hands rest. The breath she takes between tasks. He speaks with a kind of easiness that has nothing to do with being careless and everything to do with knowing what matters and what doesn't. His words land without needing to be defended. They create with a kind of clarity that seems almost reckless to someone still inside the storm, but it's not recklessness—it's specificity. They know what they're building and why. They've thought about it in silence, not in panic. They're not distracted by the need to broadcast the difficulty of building it, to perform the labor so you'll know it was costly.

The work doesn't need an explanation of how much it hurt to make. The work speaks. And because it speaks without undertone of desperation, people hear it. Your suffering was never the work's credential. It was only your insecurity posing as proof.

This is the quiet close. Not triumphant. Not revolutionary. Settled. Complete. The kind of arrival that doesn't announce itself but simply shows up in the quality of your days and the sustainability of your work and the way you can now choose who to work with and how to work and what to say yes to, because you're no longer running on the fumes of other people's expectations. You're running on your own oxygen now. It's cleaner. It lasts longer.

The last miles of a long walk are not the most exciting. They are the most honest. Your feet know the rhythm now. They move without thought. You stop thinking about the distance and start noticing the actual ground beneath you. The texture of it. Whether it's hard-packed or soft. The air. The quality of light through the trees at this hour. The bodies moving alongside you, their pace matching yours. The conversation you're having with yourself about what it all meant. Why you walked. What you were looking for. Whether you found it. What you learned that you didn't expect to learn.

And the answer, when it comes, is quiet. So quiet you might almost miss it. You found it not in some distant place, not at some imagined finish line. It was in the walking itself. In every step. In the decision to keep going even when you could barely breathe. And in the decision to stop pushing, to settle into a pace you could actually sustain. In learning the difference between those two things, and knowing now which one deserves your devotion.

You are no longer in the effort. You are after it. You've moved beyond it not by failing at it, but by completing it. And in that after-space—not wasted, not defeated, but completed—you finally start making work that only you could make. Not because you've suffered enough to earn it. But because you've grown wise enough to stop requiring suffering as permission. You stopped needing to bleed to justify your existence as a creator.

Your work no longer has to apologize for existing. It doesn't have to carry the weight of your pain, the burden of proof that you sacrificed enough. It doesn't have to justify its own value through the cost of your suffering. It can simply be what it is: a true thing, made by you, for the world you're actually in. That's everything. That's more than enough.

The struggle is behind you now. Not because it wasn't real—it was real, and it marked you, and you carry the evidence of it in every decision you make. Because you were more real than it ever was. You survived it. You learned from it. You completed the only task it had to teach you, which was to show you that you were stronger than it, and you didn't need it to be strong. And now that you've stopped proving it, everyone can finally see. Not your suffering. You. The actual person underneath the performance. That's who they wanted to see all along.

Epilogue

Ease Is Not the Enemy

The woman sits at her desk. No coffee growing cold beside her. No timer set. She writes, and the words arrive like they've been waiting in the wings all along. An hour passes. She doesn't check her phone. When she finally stops, her shoulders are still soft.

This is what you've been walking toward. Not the absence of resistance—resistance is information—but the absence of your own hand gripping your own throat.

Ease arrives quietly, which is why so many people mistake it for laziness, or drift. Laziness is passive. Ease is structural. It's what happens when you've done the invisible labor: the mapping of your own nervous system, the honest audit of what actually costs you energy, the small reversals that let you stop paying the tax on your own existence. The body knows the difference. Your hands know. The quality of attention you can hold—that knows.

Most of us learned to measure success by our own resistance. The harder something fought us, the more it proved we were serious. Conviction announced itself through suffering. We made bargains with ourselves: *When I'm exhausted enough, when I've paid enough, then I'll be allowed to do good work. Then it will matter.* But effort doesn't confer meaning. Meaning makes effort disappear.

You've spent this time learning to ask different questions. Not *How much can I endure?* but *What am I trying to say?* Not *What will convince them I'm legitimate?* but *Who actually needs this, and will my work help them find their footing?* The second set of questions doesn't lead to ease because you stop struggling. It leads to ease because you stop struggling against yourself.

Value was never a function of how close you came to breaking. It was always about orientation. A photograph that takes one hour to compose is not less valuable than one that takes eight. A piece of writing that flows from clarity is not less true than one that was extracted word by word from your own resistance. The work that helps someone—that person standing in their kitchen at midnight, uncertain how to move forward, suddenly seeing a path because of something you made—that work has already proven itself. The cost you paid to make it has nothing to do with its worth.

This is liberation wearing a strange face. It doesn't look like triumph. It doesn't come with fanfare or permission from institutions. It looks like ordinary Tuesday morning competence. Like showing up to what you actually know how to do and letting that be enough. The body settles into it. The breath opens. After years of bracing, the muscles finally understand: *We don't need to be ready for an attack that isn't coming.*

* * *

You came here wanting to believe that ease was possible. You weren't sure. The narrative was so strong—the one that said the only work worth doing was the work that cost something visible, that left marks. But you're different now. You've felt it. That strange clarity when you stopped performing effort and actually started working. When the attention became concentrated not because you were strangling it but because you'd finally stopped dividing it.

The world has not asked you to relax. Everything in the system still rewards the display of struggle. Your colleagues still email at midnight. Your industry still measures devotion in hours billed. The ambient anxiety still hums just below the surface, suggesting that ease is luck, or a luxury, or the quiet before some reckoning. But you are not required to accept their timeline.

You are allowed to create without suffering. This is not a nice idea. It is not motivational speak. It is a fact about how humans actually produce their best work, and it contradicts almost everything you were taught. The body knows what the mind still doubts. When you're not in a state of low-level panic, your ability to see problems—to actually *see*—expands. Your intuition stops being drowned out by the sound of your own resistance. You remember things you'd forgotten: how to be curious, how to stay with something difficult without immediately escalating to crisis mode, how to let a sentence breathe before you destroy it.

This takes practice. Not the practice of forcing relaxation, but the practice of noticing where you still grip, where you still half-believe that the suffering was the point. You'll catch yourself working with your jaw clenched and simply release it. You'll feel the impulse to make something harder to prove it's real, and you'll recognize it as the old language and let it pass. These moments compound. They're the difference between believing ease is possible and knowing it.

* * *

You are allowed to rest inside your competence. The competence was already there. Years of work have woven it into your cells. You know things now that you didn't know before. Your hands remember. Your instincts have been calibrated. The knowledge doesn't evaporate if you don't remind yourself constantly that you're struggling.

This is the opposite of arrogance. Arrogance is a kind of performance too—another way of proving you're serious, another way of insisting on your own legitimacy. Knowing what you know and trusting it is simply accurate. It's the position of someone who has done the work and is no longer willing to pretend it didn't happen.

The measure of skill is not how hard something looks from the outside. It's how much of your attention gets to stay free. A master reaches across the table without thinking about the mechanics of reaching. A writer doesn't monitor her breath while she writes. A teacher doesn't debate whether she has earned the right to be in the room. This is not confidence—confidence is still a performance. This is recognition. You know what you've learned. You don't have to convince anyone, including yourself.

* * *

What you make will be amplified now. The tools are here. AI does not create meaning—it cannot—but it will carry your meaning further than you could alone. It will extend the reach of the work without diminishing it. The voice is still yours. The choice of what matters is still yours. The orientation toward helping someone actually move, actually think differently, actually find ground—that comes from you. The tool is incapable of caring. So it doesn't matter if it's faster, or more efficient, or seemingly effortless. None of that transfers meaning to the work. The meaning was already yours. The technology just doesn't get in the way.

This frees you from the story that creation requires a kind of expensive artisanal suffering. Some work will always be difficult. Some problems will resist. That's different. That's the friction between what you're trying to express and the limits of the medium. That's real. But the suffering you added on top—the self-imposed doubt, the performance of struggle, the refusal to let anything be easy—that was never required. It was always a choice.

* * *

You are allowed to trust the ease. It is not a trick. It is not the quiet before collapse. It is not rest from which you will have to pay back with interest later. This is what mastery feels like from the inside.

Not the feeling of certainty. Certainty is brittle. Not the feeling of having arrived permanently. You haven't. But the feeling of knowing how to move through uncertainty without dissolving into it. Of being able to hold a question without immediately abandoning it or grabbing for the first answer. Of trusting that the work you make from clarity will be more useful than the work you make from panic, and acting on that trust.

The woman at her desk is still learning. Still surprised by what comes up in her own writing. Still encountering problems that have no obvious solution. But she's no longer at war with the fact of her own existence while trying to create. She's inside her own life, and from that position, the work can flow.

This is the conversation you've been having with yourself across these pages. Not whether you're worthy of success, not whether your voice matters, not whether you deserve to rest. You already know the answer to those questions. The real conversation has been about permission. About whether you're actually willing to stop performing effort and start creating from what you know.

The answer has always been yes. You were just waiting for someone to say it was allowed.

It is allowed. The ease is not the enemy. You are. Or rather: the part of you that still believes the suffering proves something. That part gets to rest now too. There is work to do, clarity to move toward, others waiting for what only you can make. None of it requires you to hurt yourself along the way.

Trust this. Trust the ease. Trust what your body has been trying to tell you all along: *We're ready now. We can move forward without bracing for impact. The ground is solid. It holds.*

You are allowed to believe it. And from that belief, without strain, the next thing gets made.

About The Author

Kim Aronson

Kim Aronson is a writer, teacher, and intuitive guide working at the intersection of psychology, nervous system awareness, and lived human experience.

His work focuses on the quiet patterns that shape how people relate, belong, and lose themselves, often long before they have words for what is happening. Rather than offering techniques or quick transformation, Kim's writing invites a slower kind of understanding: one that respects timing, emotional safety, and the intelligence of survival strategies formed early in life.

Alongside his writing, Kim has an intuitive reading practice where he works with individuals who feel emotionally stuck, relationally uncertain, or disconnected from their own inner authority. These sessions are less about prediction and more about orientation, helping people recognize patterns, name what they are sensing, and rebuild trust in their own perception. This work continually informs his writing, grounding it in real lives rather than abstract theory.

Kim is the author of more than one hundred books on self-development, relationships, emotional literacy, and consciousness. His approach blends psychological insight with reflective storytelling, offering language for experiences that are often felt deeply but rarely articulated clearly. His work is especially resonant with readers who are thoughtful, sensitive, and self-aware, yet still find themselves struggling with boundaries, voice, and presence in close connection.

He is also the founder of **Wisdom Publishing**, a boutique publishing company that helps thoughtful people turn lived insight into books. Wisdom Publishing supports authors through the full process of writing and publishing, with a focus on clarity, integrity, and accessible nonfiction that speaks to the inner life.

More of Kim's writing, books, and current projects can be found on his websites, where he continues to explore themes of relational honesty, emotional embodiment, and conscious self-expression.

www.KimAronson.com
www.Wisdom-Publishing.com
www.WisdomManuals.com

www.ingramcontent.com/pod-product-compliance
Lightning Source LLC
LaVergne TN
LVHW022048200926
848481LV00003B/835